IMPROVE YOUR
BOWLS

IMPROVE YOUR
BOWLS

CollinsWillow
An Imprint of HarperCollins*Publishers*

Collins Willow
an imprint of HarperCollins*Publishers*
London

All rights reserved

First published 1987
First published in paperback 1990
Reprinted 1992, 1993 and 1995
© HarperCollins*Publishers* 1990

ISBN 0 00 218362 5

Set in Melior by Ace Filmsetting Ltd, Frome, Somerset
Produced by HarperCollins Hong Kong

Contents

Play better bowls

Gone are the days when bowls could be dismissed as 'an old man's game'. Its great and still growing success as a televised sport has brought the game's skill, subtlety and drama to the attention of millions – armchair fans for whom David Bryant is a living legend, an instantly recognizable sporting superstar. And there is a host of rising young stars like the Scottish bowler Hugh Duff and the Englishman Danny Denison to ensure the future of the game as a television spectacle. Over 4 million BBC2 viewers watched David and me battling it out for the World Indoor Singles title in 1987.

The great passive interest in the sport has been parallelled by an unprecedented interest in playing it. There are today national bowling associations in twenty seven countries – with keen bowlers taking to the greens in settings as far apart as Singapore and Argentina, Spain and Papua New Guinea. Meanwhile, the game continues to grow apace in its old strongholds like the British Isles, Australia and New Zealand.

One reason for this expansion has been the rapid increase in the popularity (and availability) of the indoor game. Indoor greens provide year-round bowling in excellent conditions, while the leisure facilities generally provided – bars, lounges and so forth – make the clubs attractive social venues for couples and families. This has been reflected in the welcome establishment of mixed tournaments.

As the sport has surged ahead in popularity, so too has its character undergone something of a transformation. Social bowls continues, quite rightly, to underpin the game at the club level. But competitive bowls has become an increasingly serious matter, both amateur and professional. As the 'old man's' jibe has fallen away, bowls has attracted younger sportsmen and women who throw themselves into the sport with the enthusiasm and determination associated with golf and tennis. Twenty years ago, when I started taking a real interest in the game, a skip who sent down a really fierce delivery might have seen eyebrows raised in disapproval. Not so today. Within the laws of the game, and the canons of good sportsmanship, competition bowls is played in a spirit of steely resolution, with quarter neither asked nor given. The object of a contest is to play well and *win*.

Whatever your ambitions in bowling terms, and whatever your current standard of play, I believe you will find that *Improve Your Bowls* lives up to its title. It is not an autobiography, and emphatically not a personality book. It contains my views, drawn from my experience as a dedicated bowler, on every aspect of bowling technique and match-play tactics. I do not promise that it will make you a world champion, but if you apply the principles and instructions clearly laid out in its pages it will make you a better bowler than you are today. And the better a bowler you become, the more enjoyment you will get from the sport we love.

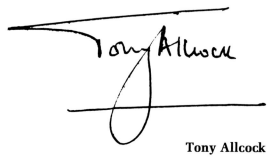

Tony Allcock

*Tony Allcock the bowler supreme —
winner of the World Indoor Singles
and Pairs titles in 1986 and 1987*

Bowls International

'The World's Number One Authority on Bowls'

In April 1981 *Bowls International* was launched on an unsuspecting public from its small offices in the picturesque market town of Stamford in South Lincolnshire.

Today *Bowls International* is recognized throughout the world as the sport's most authoritative monthly publication. Still based in Stamford, its message has spread wherever the game is played, from Worthing to Western Samoa, from Balgreen to Brisbane, from Bournemouth to Buenos Aires. In addition to keeping its readers informed of the latest developments within the flat green game, including changes in the Laws, details of television tournaments and new equipment, *Bowls International* reports on the major national and international events within the sport.

Since its inception *Bowls International* has introduced a number of innovative ideas that have established the magazine as a pacesetter in its field. In November 1981 it published the sport's first Player of the Year poll inviting readers to vote for their favourite flat and crown green personalities. As the World Indoor and Outdoor Champion of the time, David Bryant was the first recipient, with Yorkshire's Waterloo Handicap winner Roy Nicholson taking the crown title. Tony Allcock has since won the flat title on three successive occasions.

January 1982 saw the first ever publication of a Review of the Year, a fascinating comprehensive statistical listing of every country, national and international champion. This annual review is now universally recognized as the sport's most authoritative analysis.

The key to the magazine's success story is team spirit. Almost every one of *Bowls International*'s small but dedicated staff – now in demand as consultants to sponsors and manufacturers and as contributors to books, television programmes and official championship souvenir publications – is an enthusiastic bowler determined to produce a high-quality product which both informs and entertains.

However, it is in the area of bowls instruction that the magazine has really enhanced its reputation with club players at the grass roots level of the game. Most of the thanks here must go to *Bowls International*'s three major contributors – Master bowler David Bryant, English national coach Jimmy Davidson and the reigning World Indoor Champion Tony Allcock – whose combined teachings have enabled many ordinary bowlers to improve their play.

Tony Allcock has brought to the pages of *Bowls International* a wholly fresh approach to bowls instruction, and bowls enthusiasts are now fortunate enough to have a complete book of his insights and analyses. Tactics are Tony Allcock's forte, yet it is because he is also an intelligent and articulate student of bowls that he is such a fine exponent of the game. In *Improve Your Bowls* he is able to convey his good advice and helpful hints, not only through his uncanny powers of observation but also in passing on the experience he has gained playing with and against the greats in world bowls.

This long-awaited and unique book is certain to prove a favourite with bowlers of all ages and abilities throughout the world, not only for its sound advice but also for the quality of its photography, a large part of which was taken by *Bowls International*'s Duncan Cubitt, the sport's most respected photographer. That visual excellence combined with Tony Allcock's illuminating text provides an outstanding book on bowls.

Imaginative cover design, as the examples show, is one of the magazine's hallmarks.
Bowls International photographer Duncan Cubitt captures the moment, as the Queen has a spot of difficulty with Senga McCrone's hat during the presentation ceremony at the 1986 Commonwealth Games

Where there is bowls, there is Bowls International (above, at Aberdeen during the 1984 World Championships)

The editor, Chris Mills, presents Tony Allcock with his third successive Bowls International Player of the Year award in 1987

Chapter 1 **PREPARING TO BOWL**

Like any sport, bowls requires a certain amount of specialized equipment and a venue. For most players, the latter will be provided by a local or nearby club. Equipment, however, and in particular the set of bowls you decide to play with, confronts you with considerable choice. The variety of good quality bowls on the market can be quite bewildering, especially for the novice. Your aim, of course, must be to seek out the bowls that suit you best – simple enough in theory, but often quite difficult in practice. You should begin by examining the factors that govern your choice.

Choosing bowls

If you come new to the game, you face an early, indeed almost immediate decision about buying a set of bowls. They range in price from around the £60 mark to more than double that, so you will want to take what steps you can to ensure that you choose correctly. This is easier said than done, because there are many factors that have a bearing on a matter of such individuality, and it is really only by playing with a set of bowls that you will be able to judge their suitability. It is generally accepted within the game that a novice is likely to change bowls fairly early on in his or her career, because experience alone can provide a guide to genuine preference. Having said that, you are by no means reduced to buying blind first time around.

At the very outset, discuss the matter with other, experienced bowlers. Get them to explain the pros and cons of the various types of bowls they have used, and why they have settled on one in particular. Try to assess the relationship between size of hand and size and weight of bowl, and handle as many different examples as you conveniently can. When you find one that feels comfortable, ask if you can borrow the set for a brief trial. By whatever reasonable means you can, aim to reduce the field of choice, so that when you can no longer avoid committing yourself you are at least confident that your decision is as informed as you can make it. If you get it right, all well and good. If you do not, which you will know soon enough, accept the need to make a change. It would be foolish to hinder your progress and mar your enjoyment for the sake of the price of a new set of bowls.

When you actually come to buy, continue to keep an open mind within sensible limits. Go to a good sports equipment shop and handle as wide a range of bowls as you like. Do not fall into the easy trap of equating cost with suitability. It so happens that I favour the Australian-made Henselite bowls, and they are indeed at the top end of the price range. For me, they are as near as possible the perfect partner, but it does not follow that they are necessarily right for you. David Bryant uses the British-made Drakelite bowls, Willie Wood uses Drakes Pride, other top players opt for Vitalite, Concorde or Greenmaster, to name only some of the high-quality composition bowls available. Any one of these might be best for you, and it is quite conceivable that a relatively inexpensive set could suit you ideally. Be swayed by the overall 'feel' of the bowl, not by the brand name.

All these makes of bowls are available with or without grips. I favour grips myself, and have done so ever since my teenage years when I first began using competition bowls. Prior to that, I used to bowl in my back garden with an old set of lignum vitae bowls, which had belonged originally to a neighbour's grandfather. These traditional wooden bowls had no grip, but lignum vitae are now just a relic of a past age, like ivory billiard balls. As I gained experience with composition bowls, the grip came to feel natural to me, to such an extent that now I find it difficult to contemplate handling a bowl without one. Jim Baker is similarly attached to grips. Other top bowlers find the opposite to be true. David Bryant bowls without a grip, and so does Willie Wood – most of the time. Wood is unusual in this respect. Most bowlers are consistent, one way or the other. You will have to work it out for yourself, and you should be no more influenced by the fact that I like a grip than by the fact that David Bryant does not.

For what it is worth, I believe the grip has a genuine advantage in particular circumstances. Composition bowls feel rather lifeless, cold even, a bit like a tombstone on a frosty morning. Now if you really are playing on a frosty morning in October, or on a wet, windy night in May, you might well want a little more to hold on to than a naked bowl. I certainly do, and having become accustomed to using a grip for that practical reason I remain

Bowls come with or without grip, and it is entirely a matter of personal preference. Tony Allcock, for example, uses a grip while David Bryant does not. Willie Wood (right) is unusual in selecting bowls with or without grip to suit the conditions

The great David Bryant (left), as easily recognized by his delivery as by the ubiquitous pipe – after a generation at the top of the game. Sally Smith of Norfolk (above), one of the game's bright prospects

Choosing bowls

comfortable with it in circumstances that render it objectively neutral, such as the controlled conditions of an indoor green.

This leads me on to my personal views about switching bowls – choosing different sets for different circumstances. Professional bowlers are obviously in a position to have as many sets of bowls as they want, and so are you if you are prepared to stand the cost. But money aside, is it a good idea? Opinion is divided, and practice with it. David Bryant, who is not just a sporting legend but a most illuminating student of the game, uses a number of sets of bowls. When he arrives for a match he tries to read the green like a fisherman reading a trout stream. He takes into account all the relevant factors of weather, surface moisture and so forth, and then selects the set of bowls that in his judgment is the most suitable for the

Bench-testing a bowl to see that it complies with the standards set by the IBB's Master Bowl

conditions he anticipates facing in the course of the match. Given his peerless record, it would be nonsensical to argue that he is mistaken in such a policy – as it applies to his own game. But I do not follow that policy myself, and I believe that my feelings on the subject will strike a chord with the ordinary bowler. I believe, in other words, that in this respect my approach to the game is more typical of the ordinary bowler, and is therefore of greater relevance.

I believe the game should be

A selection from the many makes of composition bowls available today, along with a jack and other accessories. The bowls are all of high quality, and your choice should be governed entirely by individual preference – the bowl that feels right to you is right for you

approached in as simple a manner as possible – as simple, that is, as is compatible with the inherent complexities of an activity that rewards high technical and tactical skills. I believe in avoiding avoidable complications, and it is my considered opinion that choosing between bowls falls into that category.

A bowler does not require a vast quantity of expensive equipment, but good shoes are essential. The last thing you want is aching feet

Choosing bowls

Let me begin by making the case *for* selecting between different sets of bowls. Bowling conditions can and do show extreme variation, and this is especially true for competitors at international level. There is nothing to equal the very finest English conditions for bowling outdoors – a warm summer's day on a beautifully tended green. However, I have also bowled in Scotland with snow beginning to fall, and bowling in the rain, even driving rain, is a common, if uncomfortable, experience.

Contrast that with lightning-fast greens in Australia and New Zealand, where even a spot of rain is enough to send everyone scurrying for shelter.

Or the controlled conditions of indoor greens. It must stand to reason that, as with horses for courses, no one set of bowls is ideally suited to every situation. On a waterlogged English green the bias of any particular bowl will be much less effective than normal, so in order to play shots with your familiar line you would need a bowl with greater bias. Conversely, a fast Australian green exaggerates the bias, which would suggest selecting a bowl with less bias. Even a change in weight and size could be indicated by extreme

Rob Parrella watches David Cutler at Worthing, in ideal conditions

circumstances, and some that cannot be regarded as extreme. There is, for example, a school of thought that argues in favour of using a slightly larger bowl indoors than outdoors.

I cannot refute any of this, but I do not think it adds up to a convincing case. For me, the telling argument against it is that it can lead to confusion and distraction. In the first place you have to be able to choose unerringly. In competition bowling you are allowed a maximum of eight practice bowls before a match. How confident are you that such a limited period of experimentation will always give you the correct answer? Even the best players can get it

wrong. For a match against Jim Baker in the 1986 Superbowl tournament, Willie Wood made a choice between two sets of bowls of similar manufacture, of identical size and weight but with different biases. He brought out the set that in his opinion (his highly educated opinion, it must be remembered) better suited the conditions. Early on in the match he realized that he had read the green wrongly during his practice ends, and that the other set of bowls would in fact have suited the circumstances better. After losing the match, Wood attributed his loss at least in part to this mistake. Now if he can get it wrong at a critical time, where does that leave you?

A waterlogged green is a bowler's nightmare. The Canadian Ronnie Jones (top right) is anxious to get on with it, so he pitches in to help sweep away the excess water at Balgreen. Old rivals Jim Baker (bowling) and Willie Wood compete indoors at Manchester (right). The British climate is the indoor game's strongest ally

Choosing bowls

I would go further, and say that even if you learned how to read the conditions with the accuracy of a David Bryant, and possessed enough bowls to accommodate them all, you would still be ill-advised to do so. When you are bowling, whatever the conditions, you have quite enough to contend with mentally – your tactics, your opponent's tactics, the state of the head, the run of the green, the line and length of the shot you are about to make, the calculation of risk and so on. You need to remain composed, even under the severest pressure, and as you prepare for the shot and execute it your concentration must be unwavering. All of these things together amount to a tall order, and for my part I do not want to make it any taller than it necessarily is. I do not, on top of all that, want to be thinking about the particular bowl in my hand – about its individual bias, or whatever else may distinguish it from the bowl I was playing with the day before. Above all, if I am playing badly I do not want nagging doubts creeping into my mind about whether I have made the right choice of bowls. If I am playing badly I want to bend every effort at my command – physical, mental and emotional – towards playing better. I do not see how I can do that if I am brooding, even subconsciously, about a better set of bowls sitting uselessly in the boot of my car.

That is the negative case, if you will, against changing bowls. But I feel there is a positive case as well, a positive case for sticking with one set of bowls. I have bowled in every tournament since the end of 1985 with the same set of Henselites, which were

specially made for me in Australia. I have used them for every practice session as well. I keep a couple of sets of bowls I have used in the past as a sort of insurance policy, in case physical changes occur in me such as to make my trusty Henselites no longer appropriate to my needs. If something like that were to happen, however, I would be just as likely to have to search out a new bowl altogether as to find I could return to an old favourite. In the meantime, I will stick to my present bowls.

Brett Morley (above) takes careful aim. In Tony Allcock's opinion, bowling accurately is quite difficult enough without the added complication of selecting bowls for the occasion. Regardless of the playing conditions, he sticks loyally to one trusted set of bowls

The reason for my loyalty is a simple one. I know these bowls well, and in the sense that such things are possible I feel that they know me. They are not perfect bowls for all the circumstances I encounter, but then I am not a perfect bowler. Within our limitations, however, we work well together, and we have been through thick and thin together in all sorts of circumstances. Perhaps we even compensate for each other's shortcomings now and again, and if that appears fanciful I will settle for the claim that these particular bowls are the best allies I have in my profession. That is the bottom line. When I hold them in my hand they feel wonderfully familiar, and the reassurance that gives me far outweighs any technical deficiencies they may have under particular circumstances.

My bowls are size 5 and of heavy weight (they could be medium or heavy). I have reasonable sized hands and could probably handle a size 6 bowl ($5\frac{1}{16}$ inches), but I do not subscribe to the school of thought that you should use the very largest bowl that you can comfortably handle. The theoretical advantage of the larger bowl (the larger the better) is that it cuts a wider swathe through the head, and is therefore more likely to connect with an object bowl – to advance it, or knock it around or whatever your intention may be. If you imagine extreme differences of size, like a football and a golf ball, this could not be more apparent. In the reality of bowling, however, the size differences can only be marginal, and a sixteenth of an inch here or there can only have a marginal effect.

An extract from the IBB Laws of the Game, indicating the range of bowl sizes permitted.

Size in inches	Size Number	Actual Metric (mm)	May be rounded off Metric (mm)
4-5/8	0	117.4	117
4-3/4	1	120.7	121
4-13/16	2	122.2	122
4-7/8	3	123.8	124
4-15/16	4	125.4	125
5	5	127.0	127
5-1/16	6	128.6	129
5-1/8	7	130.2	130

If size numbers are utilized and size measurements omitted, then no Bowl in diameter shall be less than 4-5/8 inches (117.4mm) nor more than 5-1/8 inches (130.2mm) and no Bowl shall weigh more than 3lb 8oz (1.59kg).

Choosing bowls

Against that must be set the fact that your maximum comfortable size under ideal circumstances may become decidedly uncomfortable under difficult circumstances, and I think it is wise to keep a little bit in reserve. Most bowlers in Britain bowl outdoors all or most of the time. They must take the conditions as they find them, and they are often far from ideal to put it mildly. Therefore, I think it sensible to select a size that remains comfortable and easily controllable under adverse conditions. If you want to know what they are, or at least to approximate them, run your bowling hand under the cold tap until it is thoroughly chilled. Then dry it and take a bowl out of the refrigerator. The way the bowl feels in your hand is the way it is going to feel on plenty of occasions when you are playing. (Incidentally, beware of leaving your bowls in the car boot for any length of time before a match. Composition bowls take an eternity to warm up, and you may have lost your match before they do!)

The danger of using a bowl that is too large for you, even a shade too large under the worst conditions, is that you will find yourself stretching to grip it, and then when you come to release it you may find that it has a tendency to slide out of your hand as if by its own volition rather than by yours. Controlled release is obviously critical to accurate delivery, and anything that endangers it can only be detrimental.

Choosing a bowl for size and weight is comparatively straightforward, because those factors are directly influenced by your physical

particularities. Choosing for running characteristics, or bias, involves more subtle calculations, if indeed it is a matter of calculation at all. There is an international testing bowl which under controlled conditions (bench test) describes the minimum allowable arc. All bowls must be similarly bench-tested before being approved, and they must not show less bias. Beyond that, they can have any desired degree of bias (even if, confusingly, they are all stamped Bias 3).

'Welcome to Edinburgh' indeed! The women from Hong Kong and Fiji found the inclement weather during the 1986 Commonwealth Games not to their liking

The range of performance between a fairly straight-running bowl (near the minimum) and a really wide-running, or bending bowl is great, and your choice here will deeply affect the way you play your shots. Many players scorn the straight-running bowl on the grounds that

Choosing bowls

minimizing the arc reduces the skill involved, and that it somehow detracts from the essential flavour of the game. I think this is cant, and would advise you to ignore any such prejudice. If you can bowl more successfully with a straight-running bowl then use it, although you should be aware that its attractions imply corresponding disadvantages. The straighter the line from A to B, the greater the chance for accuracy. On the other hand, that accuracy is of little use if the circumstances of play are such that an intervening bowl is blocking your desired path. At the other extreme, a heavily biased bowl can look quite majestic as it takes its wide arc into the head, and because it can take advantage of the whole width of the green it can in theory get around all manner of obstacles. However, to control its journey with anything like pinpoint accuracy is extremely difficult.

Playing conditions can have a dramatic effect on a bowl's natural bias, and this too exposes the limitations of the extremes. A slow, soggy green inhibits the bias, which further restricts the minimum-bias bowl. The hard, very fast Australian and New Zealand greens exaggerate bias, and it would be suicidal to bowl on them with a really swinging bowl. I would say that if there is a telling case ever to be made for changing bowls, it lies here. I suspect that those players who prefer to follow that policy will tend to restrict their change to bias, retaining the same size and weight. My bowls are medium bias, which means that they are as well equipped as any one set can be to accommodate play-

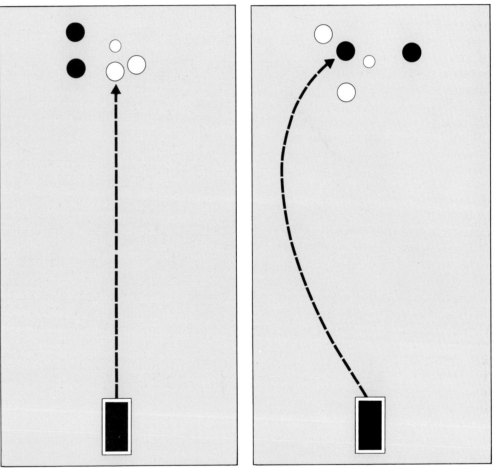

While a bowl will never travel the length of the rink in a perfectly straight line, a combination of extreme pace and heavy conditions very nearly neutralizes the bias

The faster the green and the slower the pace, the greater the degree of bias. On the fastest New Zealand greens, for example, a bowl played with draw weight almost seems to approach the jack finally at a right angle to it

ing conditions at both ends of the spectrum.

From my observation, most players at any level of the game incline towards medium bias, but there are enough successful exceptions to leave the question open. Neil Thompson, a long-serving number 2 in the England indoor team, uses heavily biased bowls to great effect. However, on occasion I cannot help feeling that these bowls subject his excellent technique to quite a fearsome testing – one that I would choose to avoid myself. For example, during the 1986 Home International indoor series we were playing against Wales in Swansea, and the green was extremely fast and swinging. Thompson was taking twice as much green as anybody else, and while he bowled very well he must, in my opinion, have been labouring under something of a disadvantage. Of course he knows those bowls as well as I know mine, and I can easily understand his unwillingness to be parted from them, whatever the objective conditions. Wynne Richards, too, chooses to bowl with a wide arc, and the fact that he has twice won the England outdoor singles title should stop anyone from being dogmatic about bias.

In the light of all these permutations of size, weight, grip and bias, some argue in favour of a greater degree of standardization. Size and weight must obviously be allowed variety, but there is no reason in principle why the bias could not be standardized – or at least nearly standardized. Two different manufacturers would find it impossible to achieve absolutely identical bias; and

even bowls of one manufacturer differ slightly. The argument runs that by insisting on bowls that are as near as possible uniform, individual technical and tactical skill will under no circumstances be obscured by superiority of equipment, and will therefore be more appropriately rewarded. There may be an element of truth in that, but I do not think it will ever be put into effect. It is hard to imagine thousands, indeed millions, of bowlers willingly scrapping their bowls in the interests of what critics would consider obsessive tidy-mindedness. I hope I am right about this, because I think the current variety of choice adds richness and interest to the game.

Neil Thompson of England prefers a heavily biased bowl. He is a fine player, but Tony Allcock thinks his choice of bowls exaggerates the difficulty of coping with fast greens

Equipment and clothing

Apart from the set of bowls you originally (or eventually) settle on, the most important item of equipment is a pair of good bowling shoes. You are always on your feet during a match, and it would be a false economy to skimp on something that can make the difference between feeling comfortable and suffering sore feet. I know that from my younger days, when a couple of hours in cheap shoes would leave me thinking about my aching feet when I should have been concentrating completely on my bowling. Buy leather shoes, and buy good ones. They last for a long time.

It is a source of minor irritation to me and others that UK governing bodies prohibit the use of all-white shoes, such as are routinely used in Australia and New Zealand. The main reason given for prohibiting them is that, if someone were standing behind the jack in white shoes, the white on white might confuse the bowler's vision. From my experience of playing in white shoes in Australia and New Zealand, I give this no credence at all, and it is my hope that one day the regulation will be relaxed. White shoes look smarter than brown, and I believe that even such a trivial thing can have an influence on the game. Everyone seems to agree, for example, that the elegant attire of snooker players has had at least some bearing on its phenomenal television appeal. As far as we British bowlers are concerned, the only occasions on which we are allowed to wear white shoes in this country is when we are competing against players from other countries – when we are playing under regulations set down by either the International Bowling Board or the World Indoor Bowls Council. It would be good to see standardization on this.

While our cousins in Australia and New Zealand have the luxury of being able to scorn this advice, British bowlers must take wet gear seriously. Good quality wet gear is important for the obvious reason that you must try to keep reasonably warm and dry without unduly restricting movement. Try to get the balance right here. If it is cold as well as rainy, it is no use just putting on wet gear

White shoes are not permitted by the English Bowling Association, but they have become a familiar and attractive sight on television. From the left, David Cutler, John Bell and Rodney McCutcheon

over a shirt in order to keep your action free. You will still be freezing cold. A jumper, windcheater and wet gear should still leave you with adequate freedom.

For the rest, equipment simply consists of white trousers and shirts — like cricket. At least that is so for men. For women, the regulations are more stringent. Their skirts must fall a specified length below the knee, and they must be pleated in a specific manner. They also must wear white hats of specified size and design. Such requirements will probably strike the outside observer as either an endearing or an obnoxious relic of the past, and there are many within the game who consider them unnecessarily rigid. Perhaps we will sooner or later see some relaxation of these standards, as well as others that hardly square with contemporary notions of sexual equality. For example, many clubs (including mine) are all-male bastions. Wives are in evidence when it comes to making and serving tea and cucumber sandwiches, but not on the bowling green. Or one could consider an anomaly that cropped up during the 1986 McCarthy and Stone national mixed pairs, which was the first outdoor mixed competition to be conducted under national auspices. According to national rules, men are permitted to smoke on the green but women are not. Amongst the competitors was a husband and wife team, both of whom were heavy smokers. They both smoked on the green, him quite legally, her flouting the rules. I am not aware of any other organized activity in which that could happen.

Bowling clubs

The game of bowls is much more tightly linked to the institution of the bowling club than is the case with, say, tennis. You will, now and again, find people bowling in public parks (probably with rather useless cast-off lignum bowls provided by the park-keeper), but on nothing like the scale that you see people playing on public tennis courts. A great many, perhaps even most, social tennis players never play anywhere but on public courts, which means that etiquette over such matters as dress, sexual parity and the like need not concern them. With bowls, on the other hand, you are most likely to be involved with a club, with all that entails, right from day one.

There is a rich diversity of bowling clubs in Britain, from intimate little village clubs through to those large clubs that provide a competitive environment for the most committed players. There is a direct parallel here with cricket, and as with cricket the village club is a treasured institution, and as good a place as any for the aspiring youngster to develop his skills. My early days in the game were spent in such a club – the Fosseway Bowling Club in Syston, Leicestershire. It was a marvellous club, not least because of the welcome they extended to a fourteen-year-old who was falling in love with the game. If you decide to enjoy your bowls purely as a social activity, you cannot improve on such a club.

Within two or three years, however, I was beginning to win a number of local competitions, and I realized that if I wanted to take on stiffer challenges then I needed the more competitive environment of a larger club. Naturally enough, better players tend to congregate, and they do so in the larger clubs. My club in Cheltenham, one of the largest in the country, boasts three internationals. Mike Jordan, Roger Turley and I have all been capped for England, and when we put out our Challenge Cup team each of us will take a rink. It follows that aspiring young players – the champions of the future – will be drawn to such a club in order to experience the toughest competition around.

It would be difficult to imagine a more typical looking venue than the Royal Household Bowling Club at Windsor

Mavis Steele, whose achievements in the women's game are legendary, is an interesting exception to this tendency. For many years while she was at the very top of the international game she persisted in playing at a tiny little Middlesex club, which I believe had no more than a dozen members. She was simply happy there, and one would want no better reason than that. Bowls is supposed to be enjoyable, at whatever level, and the delights of village bowling form an important part of my personal experience.

The Grattons Bowling Club, Sussex (right), is a good example of the modern indoor club, providing excellent playing conditions. Motcombe Gardens, Eastbourne (below), provides a classic urban backdrop to the summer game

Chapter 2 THE ART OF DELIVERY

From the moment you step on to the mat, you should be concentrating on a single goal – to deliver the bowl perfectly so as to achieve your desired result. The mat is not the place to ponder shot selection, but to execute the shot selected. You are therefore in the realms of pure bowling technique. The grip and stance are means to an end – a smooth, consistent action accurately measured in line and length.

Gripping the bowl

Holding a bowl in preparation for delivery might seem a straightforward enough proposition, but in fact it is a subject on which players hold strong, conflicting views. The fundamental choice is between resting the bowl in the palm of the hand (the cradle grip) and holding it further forward in the fingers, with the thumb moving towards the top of the bowl (the claw grip, or, if the bowl is completely clear of the palm, the finger grip).

The cradle grip, with the hand cupped and the thumb dropped, enjoys considerable favour in the UK because it allows you to gain maximum power with minimum effort. It therefore suits heavy conditions, and it can also compensate for certain physical drawbacks – weak, or simply small hands. Under normal circumstances I use the cradle grip, although my hands are neither weak nor small. I do, however, alter my grip to cope with the conditions that prevail.

David Bryant and many other players consider the claw grip to be the best all-purpose grip. The thumb is placed along the grip-line of the bowl, which comes forward out of the palm of the hand and rests on the fingers. The claw grip's advocates claim that it makes for more sensitive

Tony Allcock demonstrates the cradle grip (above) – with the bowl resting comfortably in the palm of the hand, and the thumb gripping the side of the bowl. Welshman Terry Sullivan (left) shows how the cradle grip looks from the other side

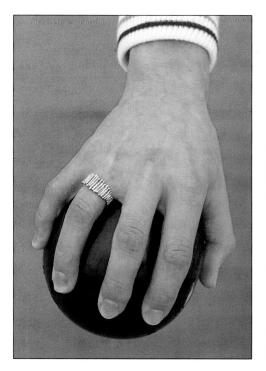

An underview of Tony Allcock's cradle grip (above), showing the dropped thumb

Three views of the claw grip (right), showing the fundamental differences between it and the cradle grip – the bowl resting forward in the fingers and the thumb raised towards the top of the bowl. David Bryant, in fact, is holding the bowl so far forward, and with the thumb so raised, that it is approaching the finger grip

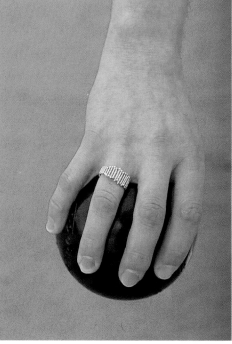

Gripping the bowl

control, and that simply by varying the pressure on the bowl it becomes relatively easy to adjust the weight of shot (depending upon the requirements of the particular shot and the pace of the green).

The finger grip is an extreme version of the claw, where the bowl lies well forward in the fingers and the thumb near the top, inside the rings. It is very popular in Australia and New Zealand, although it is generally considered unsuited to the heavier UK conditions. It allows maximum sensitivity and touch when playing the most delicate shots (for example, drawing on the fastest greens), and the thumb position tends to cut down the bias, which is useful when driving on very fast surfaces. With all grips, the fingers should be parallel to the running base of the bowl, and it is important to prevent the little finger from straying to the side of the bowl.

Tony Allcock demonstrates the finger grip. The bowl is almost entirely held by fingers and thumb, with the thumb having come right to the top. This grip is particularly suited to very fast greens, and is therefore popular in Australia and New Zealand

Argentina's Clemente Bausili about to deliver from the finger grip (far left), in competition against Tony Allcock. England manager Mal Hughes (left) gives BBC television presenter David Icke a few tips. For this shot, Icke is uncompromisingly committed to the cradle grip

Bowls is eminently suited to disabled participants, even the wheelchair-bound. The delivery is restricted to arm and shoulder, but indoor conditions are undemanding in terms of sheer power – allowing this bowler to execute his shot with a claw grip

Stance and delivery

There are basically three types of stance from which a bowl can satisfactorily be delivered: the athletic or upright, the crouch, and the fixed. Each has its devotees amongst good players, although by no means in equal numbers, and you will soon discover the one that suits you best.

The athletic stance is by far the most common, and it is the one I use. It has always seemed to me the most natural method of bowling, or, to universalize the action, of rolling a ball. Give a toddler an orange from the sideboard, and if he has a mind to roll it he will simply bend his knees and away it goes across the floor. The upright stance is really as simple as that. You just stand comfortably on the mat, feet in line with the shot, aim, bend your knees, step forward with the leg opposite your bowling arm and release the bowl. Some players modify the athletic stance somewhat by bending both back and knees before going into the delivery motion. I tend to be fairly upright, although I do actually bend my knees slightly and lower my head before delivery.

The crouch stance has been immortalized by David Bryant, and, along with the pipe, it is his most visibly distinctive characteristic. Many players use a crouch stance, although the degree of crouch varies. Bryant crouches deeply, with his legs fully bent and his entire body weight on the backs of his legs. He finds it comfortable, and he says that it improves the accuracy of his line. It is of course impossible actually to deliver a bowl from a deep crouch, which is in effect a sort of preliminary to the delivery proper. You will notice that Bryant

Tony Allcock demonstrates the true athletic stance – upright, feet in line with the shot, with the natural bending and striding motion to follow

One of the world's leading women bowlers, Margaret Johnston of Ireland, prepares to deliver from the semi-athletic stance. The knees and back are bent, but the actual delivery is as it would be from the true athletic stance

rises from the crouch to a greater or lesser extent depending upon the type of shot he is playing. When he is playing the draw, he rises no more than he has to in order to deliver the bowl comfortably with sufficient weight to reach the jack. When he is playing with medium strength he rises higher, and when he wants to fire one he comes nearly upright in the course of the delivery. Whatever the type of delivery and depth of crouch, the forward stride is the same as it is with the upright stance, which means that in its essentials the crouch is a variation of the upright. It therefore shares the upright stance's major advantage over any fixed stance, which is that the delivery action is a combination of forward body movement and swinging arm movement. This allows for maximum controllable power, without the necessity for exaggerated backswing.

The fixed stance is in marked contrast. The bowler takes up his position on the mat with his left foot (assuming he is right-handed) down the line of delivery. In a truly fixed stance, the left foot has completed its full step before the delivery begins. If it is only partly down the line, with the full step to be completed during the delivery, it is called a semi-fixed stance. The free hand is used to stabilize the body by grasping the knee or thigh of the leading leg.

I do not recommend a fixed stance for a normally fit player. It has a notional advantage in that by placing the foot forward you are effectively pre-selecting the line, and should in theory be pretty certain of delivering along that line. That guarantee, if

Bill Moseley of South Africa preparing to deliver from the semi-fixed stance – the forward stride partially completed, and the free hand bracing the knee

The famous Bryant crouch, with the legs fully bent and the body weight completely on the backs of the legs. He rises to make the delivery, but finds this preliminary crouch helps him with his line

Stance and delivery

such it is, is not available with the upright stance, where planting the foot down the line of delivery is an active part of the entire delivery. The problem with a fixed stance is that because the step has been taken, or partly taken, the natural weight transference which provides momentum during the course of delivery is drastically curtailed. So, too, is follow-through. The net effect is to place almost the entire burden of the delivery on the arm and shoulder. If the shot does not require much power, that burden is manageable, but as you try to step up the power you will readily understand the limitations of a fixed stance. If you need to fire one in heavy conditions your backswing will be desperately overloaded, and you will face grave difficulties in controlling it.

My firm preference for the upright stance, in any of its variations, assumes normal fitness. Bowlers with a greater or lesser degree of physical disability may have no alternative to a fixed stance, and some handicapped bowlers manage to employ it to great effect. During the 1970s I used to win many competitions in partnership with the fine Leicestershire bowler Bill Smith. He had suffered polio as a child, and as a consequence he had been forced to develop a most unorthodox fixed stance. He planted himself firmly on the mat, took his full step and then locked his hand on his thigh with his fingers pointing towards the inside of his leg and his elbow jutting out to the front and side. The effect was to form almost a square of upper arm, forearm, thigh and torso, and it gave him a rock-solid

base from which to deliver his bowl. Admittedly he struggled on heavy outdoor greens, but on fast indoor surfaces he displayed the most marvellous touch. Once bolted into position he had nothing to concern himself with except the grooved action of his bowling arm, and a sweetly grooved action it was, the arm swinging like a pendulum from the shoulder.

That pendulum action is the key to a controlled, flowing delivery, from whatever stance. During the delivery the shoulder, upper arm, elbow, forearm, wrist and bowl should all move as one, along the aiming line. In common with other sports that involve putting a ball into motion (like golf and snooker), you must make certain not to raise your head until the bowl has safely left your hand. There must be nothing jerky in the delivery, and a smooth follow-through should be its natural final component. That follow-through can be as languid as Bryant's or as brisk as mine (two absolute extremes), but it must round off the action. My follow-through is a coach's nightmare, but within the context of my delivery it is a wholly natural one. That is, it is natural to me, not to you, in all likelihood, and is therefore not to be copied. I doubt if it shall ever appear in a coaching manual!

The part of my action that might appear, however, if only as a footnote, is the motion of the right arm up to the point of delivery. Conventionally, the palm of the hand faces up the green throughout the backswing and delivery. In order to keep the backswing in a perfectly straight line, it is necessary to pivot the hips slightly as the

A jack's eye view of Tony Allcock's delivery. As Tony begins his backswing he starts to rotate his wrist, eventually taking the bowl through 180 degrees as the hand swings past the leg sideways on both during the backswing and the delivery. This action, which Tony picked up from David Bryant, allows the bowler to bring his arm through on a perfectly straight line. If you can take to it naturally you might find it as useful as they do. But if you find it forced, content yourself with the more conventional delivery favoured by the vast majority of bowlers

Stance and delivery

step is taken and the arm comes through. That is the way I bowled at the beginning, and it is the way the vast majority of bowlers have always bowled. However, David Bryant, always the innovator, has developed a radically different way of bringing the bowling arm through, and once I understood the theory and found that it worked for me in practice I became a convert. Bryant had observed that when the arm moves freely beside the leg, as in walking, the palm automatically faces the side of the leg. It feels entirely natural to have the palm outstretched when your arm is out in front of you, just as it feels natural to have the palm facing upwards when your arm is stretched out behind you, but when it swings past your leg, its only natural position is side on. From this observation, Bryant was able to develop an absolutely smooth, tension-free delivery that involved a 180-degree turn of the wrist. The bowl comes through a ninety-degree

turn from the extended backswing to the rest position (as it passes the leg), and then through another ninety degrees from there to release, at which point the palm is facing up the green just as it is with the conventional delivery. Bryant argues that this is the only possible way of combining a perfectly straight backswing with keeping the body square to the aiming line (thereby avoiding the slight body pivot).

This is demonstrably true, and you can easily prove it to yourself by following Bryant's simple demonstration. Stand with your feet together and take both arms back simultaneously with the palms facing forward. Then swing them both forward to the full extent. As they pass the rest position they begin to curve outwards, ending up at a noticeable angle from the body. There is therefore no way of bringing either arm on its own through straight without pivoting the body. Now attempt the same exercise

using the 180-degree twist with both wrists. You will automatically come through on a straight line. This conclusively proves the theory, but that is not sufficient reason to adopt the style. I have done so because it feels perfectly natural and comfortable.

If it did not, I would bowl in the conventional manner as almost all top bowlers do. I have seen many players labouring to perform the Bryant twist, to coin a phrase, with results that border on the grotesque. Unless you can take to it naturally, so that it becomes completely unconscious, you are advised to forget it. That is a part of a wider truth that cannot be emphasized too strongly. Everything in bowls depends upon your ability to perform your delivery action smoothly and consistently, time after time after time. Experiment as much as you like with various techniques, but in the final analysis you must adopt only those elements that do not require forcing, only those

Midway through the backswing, Tony Allcock's weight has been transferred completely to the right foot, while the left foot has come off the mat and started its forward stride

The complete Allcock delivery. It is a perfectly natural series of movements, from the controlled backswing through to grounding the bowl. At that point, Tony habitually snatches his hand away where most other players follow through in a more leisurely manner. He does not recommend that you copy this curious mannerism!

Stance and delivery

elements that can be incorporated seamlessly into your natural individual style. A good delivery action is a case of total design, where the whole is greater than the sum of the parts.

The enormous variety in bowling styles – successful bowling styles – is a curiosity. If you consider other still-ball sports, the top players tend towards uniformity in actual technique, however much they may vary in those peripheral matters that make them easily identifiable as individuals. You could hardly confuse the golfers Greg Norman and Lee Trevino, even at a distance, but if you looked at their respective driving actions in slow motion they would look at least similar. Steve Davis and Jimmy White are radically different types of snooker player, but in fact they both have textbook cue actions, as do virtually all the good players.

This simply is not the case with bowls – with all its variety of grips, stances and delivery actions. You can find really good players who possess a classic action – pretty well perfect in every particular and therefore extremely pleasing to the eye. The New Zealander Peter Belliss has such an action. From the relaxed ease of the backswing to the flowing grace of the follow-through, his delivery is simply lovely. If you can successfully pattern your action on his, then you will not only bowl very elegantly but very well too. You would certainly be better advised to emulate his action than David Bryant's or mine.

Bryant exaggerates both backswing and follow-through to a remarkable degree, and as far as I am concerned

Peter Belliss of New Zealand (here competing against Dennis Katunarich of Australia) has a most elegant delivery action – with a smooth follow-through

The Allcock follow-through. Sometimes Tony appears almost to snatch his hand away at the moment of delivery – as if he cannot wait to be rid of the bowl. This is a classic example of the personalized nature of successful bowling technique. It obviously works well for him – which is no indication that it would work for you

he is literally inimitable (unless you want to risk doing a parody). As for my release and follow-through (if indeed you can call it that), well might you scratch your head. Why do I snatch my hand away, as though I were holding a hot potato? Have I some secret entry into the mysteries of the game, unknown to anyone else, that might be unlocked to you if you could adopt the same technique? Do not even think about it. There is nothing to recommend that part of my action except that it clearly works for me. It has been with me for a long time, and probably emerged in my days of back-garden bowling, where I recollect being in a terrible hurry to bowl as many bowls as possible. I have never attempted to correct my quick-fire release in the sense of making it more orthodox, because during my adult career I have never suffered a prolonged slump in my fortunes. I succeed well enough despite this 'fault', and do not really think I would succeed better if I 'cured' it.

I believe there are two reasons for such a lack of standardization in bowling technique. First, there is enormous variation in greens in the UK, and, depending upon where you learn to play, your technique will be influenced by the conditions you find yourself contending with. Greens in the Southern Hemisphere show nothing like the same variety, and neither do the players in terms of technique. Second, it must be in large part attributable to the fact that most of today's top bowlers, including comparatively younger ones like me, learned the game in an era before the establishment of serious coaching

Stance and delivery

schemes of the sort we now have. I received no coaching of any sort, and if I had there is no doubt that my action would have been sorted out (for better or worse). Presumably, coaching on a wide scale will result in a measure of standardization – at least to the extent of curbing the more extreme idiosyncrasies – but it would be a shame if bowling technique became uniform. Good coaching should encourage natural talents, not stifle individuality, and I would never like to see the day when the gifted natural player is at the mercy of the manufactured article.

Take the matter of what to do with your back foot during delivery. In Britain, it is normal to lift the foot off the mat. In Australia and New Zealand it is normal to keep it anchored to the mat. This is entirely because of the normal condition of greens in the two environments. You will automatically get more power into the shot if you lift the foot because by doing so you accelerate the forward momentum as you bend into the delivery. In Britain you tend to need the extra

Wendy Line of Hampshire, the 1986 Commonwealth Games Singles Gold Medallist, follows through in the conventional manner. The back leg has come clear of the mat as a natural part of the body's forward momentum

power, emphatically so under really heavy conditions. Scottish bowlers in particular develop the habit of putting their bodies behind their bowls, pressing forward to gain maximum controlled power through the delivery. Willie Wood, George Adrain and the great Willie McQueen are conspicuous examples of this, and it is a direct consequence of their having learned to bowl in the heaviest conditions known to bowlers.

One might think that a technique developed for conditions at one end of the spectrum would prove an insurmountable handicap when applied at the other, but not so. Willie Wood won the Commonwealth Games title in Brisbane in 1982 on extremely fast greens, and he did so without altering his delivery. He was still leaning right into the bowl, but he somehow managed to control the weight exceptionally well. I cannot believe that he would have achieved such a result had he tried to make the major alteration in his style that would have been necessary to adapt it properly to the conditions.

David Corkill of Northern Ireland follows through with his back foot still in contact with the mat (left). This has the effect of throttling back on the power of the shot, and it is therefore a technique much favoured in the playing conditions of the Southern Hemisphere, where the greens tend to be extremely fast. The Allcock sequence below shows the follow-through for a real power shot – the body right forward and the back leg coming high off the mat

Line and length

Grip, stance and the various mechanical aspects of delivery are all means to an end: the end is to place the bowl where you want to place it, no more and no less. Line and length, in combination, are the essence of the game. Assuming that you have an adequate grasp of the tactics of the game, and these are not difficult to acquire, it will be your mastery of line and length that will determine your fortunes.

Whatever the weight of shot you are playing, the key to getting the correct line is to assess with accuracy the point on the green at which the bowl will begin to curve in towards the objective. This point is sometimes referred to as the shoulder of the arc — that is, the point outermost from a straight line that the bowl takes on its journey. This point is generally between two-thirds and three-fifths of the way between mat and jack (assuming the jack is the objective). If you can correctly gauge the shoulder of the arc, working backwards from the target, then you have by definition got the right line.

All bowlers would agree up to this point, but when it comes to the practice of aiming to deliver along the selected line the technique varies. Some like to extend the line to a point on the bank, and aim at that. Others bring the line back to a point fairly close to the mat, and aim at that. In theory there should be no difference, since the bias will take effect at the shoulder of the arc regardless of the notional aiming point. I have always found it easier to focus my attention on what I imagine to be the shoulder of the arc and aim for that point itself,

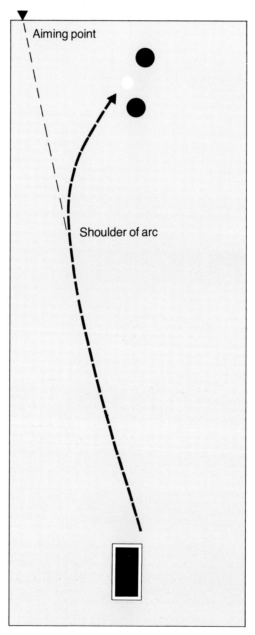

Some bowlers (David Bryant is one) mentally extend the line from the imagined shoulder of the arc to a point on the bank behind the ditch, and aim for that

rather than one either closer or further along the line.

I trained myself to do this using a handkerchief. I used to throw the jack up, and then place a handkerchief on the spot I considered to be the shoulder of the arc in order to draw to the jack. I would then bowl over the handkerchief. If I had placed the handkerchief correctly (assuming the bowl was correctly weighted) I would draw to the jack. The handkerchief could then be adjusted when bowling to a different length.

That handkerchief remains with me even today, at least in my imagination. I assess the line, look along that line for the shoulder of the arc, place the handkerchief there and then aim for it.

However you take your point of aim, when the moment of delivery comes that point is only one of two that will concern you. The other is the objective itself, whether it is the jack or another bowl or whatever. Which of the two do you look for at the final moment, as the bowl leaves your hand? David Bryant is adamant about this. He says that you must focus on your aiming point, that the objective (the jack, say) is an irrelevant distraction, since it is only by ensuring accurate delivery along your (correctly chosen) line of aim that you will get to your objective. If at the last moment you divert your attention (your eyes) to the objective, you risk missing the line, and therefore the shot.

On a theoretical level I cannot quarrel with this, and for all I know it is what most good bowlers automatically do. It is not, however, the way I deliver a bowl myself. As I prepare for the shot my eyes flicker back and forth between aiming point and objective, but at the very last moment, as I actually release the bowl, I look to the objective, confident that having launched my delivery along the point of aim, so the bowl will travel. Perhaps I am trying to will the bowl to the point of my gaze, the objective, but whether my reason is conscious or subconscious, that is what I do, and have always done.

All considerations of line apply impartially to forehand and backhand deliveries. In both cases you must play absolutely straight from shoulder to bowl along the line of aim, with the right foot pointing directly along that line. You may, as many do, find the backhand shot easier to control initially. That is because the bowling arm stays tighter to the leg when bowling backhand (as the arm is brought across the body), and therefore it is less prone to wandering. The forehand action is more exposed to the vagaries of poor technique because it is taking the arm out and away from the body. It is easier for the 'pendulum' to swing erratically. If you find that you do have this common preference for the backhand you must work on your forehand until that preference is gone. It is an unacceptable liability to have to consider such a thing when selecting your shot.

Unless a particular green gives the lie to it, you can assume that the backhand line will be a mirror image of the forehand line. If you, as a right-hander, happen to be playing with a left-hander, do not make the mistake of thinking that your backhand line

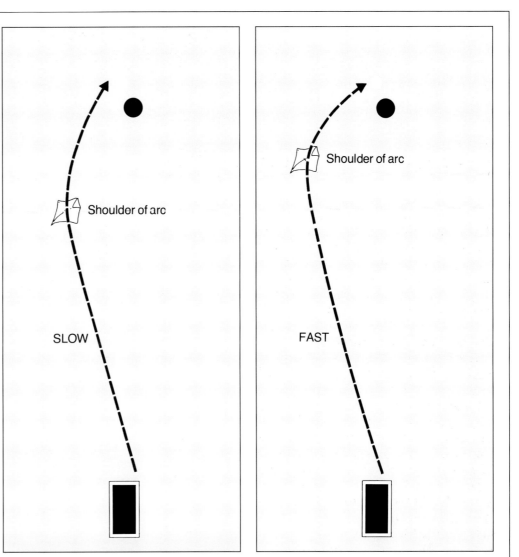

Tony Allcock's imaginary handkerchief, which he places on what he thinks is the shoulder of the arc and then bowls over. The position of the shoulder of the arc will vary depending on the green speed – nearer the mat and narrower, the slower the green. The American 'Skippy' Arculli (left) takes careful aim

will follow his forehand line. His forehand and your backhand will go down the same side of the rink, but that is where the similarity ends. The two shots are coming from completely different starting points and they will therefore follow quite different lines.

Length

In my experience, both as player and observer, length presents more problems than line. If you gain proficiency in this area, on all surfaces and in varying conditions, then you are bound to be a useful bowler.

I used to practise endlessly to perfect my length. For example, I would leave the jack off the rink and bowl instead to an imaginary line running horizontally across the green. Or I would bowl to a reasonably full length and then try to take the weight off gradually on succeeding bowls – yard by yard, foot by foot. Then, to practise line and length together, I would just scatter a few jacks at random, and then attempt a single draw shot at each. You will find that a most revealing test of your abilities, and you should persevere with it. It was by practising in such a way on as wide a variety of surfaces as I could find that I gained my skill, and, just as important, my confidence.

In dealing with problems of length caused by the most extreme bowling conditions, the back foot can be brought into play. In the UK, we usually lift the back foot off the mat during delivery. This gives us as much controlled power as we can smoothly get. I have found on occasion in the Southern Hemisphere that I need to reduce the strength of shot more than I can comfortably do with such a delivery. I have therefore, with profit, copied the locals and kept my back foot on the mat during delivery. This has the effect of throttling back on the power.

Tony Allcock prepares to practise bowling to a length (left) – in his view the most challenging technical aspect of the game. In this practice routine (right), he is bowling to different length jacks. In order to cope with the problems posed by the fastest Australian and New Zealand greens, Tony sometimes keeps his back foot on the mat throughout the delivery (below). This helps him to keep to a length, when otherwise he would have difficulty in not over-shooting

The draw shot (and variations)

The draw shot is the basis of the game of bowls, as much so for the professional as it is for the novice. Most of the time the target for a draw shot is the jack, but the target may be elsewhere in the head – another bowl or simply a given position. The definition of a draw shot, therefore, is one in which the bowl is played up the green so as to come to rest in a desired position, or as near as possible to that position.

The importance of acquiring skill at the draw shot goes beyond its obvious application. All other shots, without exception, depend upon a knowledge of the draw shot. Whatever the conditions, there is a particular line and length to draw to a particular position. Any other shot will require modifications – less green, more weight, whatever. The more or less is always in relation to the draw, and it follows that unless you know what the draw is you are hardly equipped to make rational modifications. Good bowling and indifferent drawing are therefore contradictions in terms. You must become competent at the draw shot and you should aim to master it.

Practice is essential, but in playing terms the ideal way to gain experience of drawing is to play lead in a team. The lead has no other playing function except to draw his two bowls as close to the jack as possible. There can be no better grounding in bowls than that. You may sometimes find it frustrating to play end after end in the lead, carefully drawing to the jack only to find an opponent down the order scattering your bowls to the winds. If so, just grit your teeth and persevere. Once you have gained skill and consistency with the draw shot you will feel at home in any team position, and experience will show you that it is the well-judged, well-executed draw shot above anything else in the game that marks out winners from losers.

My own skill at drawing has fluctuated over my years as a player. Ini-

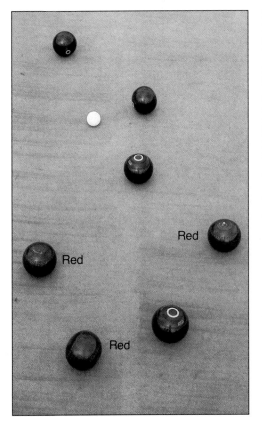 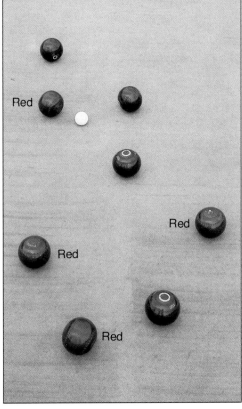

The draw shot is the cornerstone of bowls. Here, red's final bowl transforms a three-shot deficit to a one-shot advantage

tially, with all that handkerchief practice, I became extremely good at it, and won the Leicestershire singles title on three occasions mainly on my strength as a draw player. Then, in team play, I found myself moving further and further towards the back, where I concentrated on the other shots. Without doubt, my draw shot became less dependable. The skill became rusty with disuse. More recently I have made a deliberate effort to rectify this. Through practice, which I do not particularly relish, I believe I have brought my draw shot to as high a standard as I ever achieved in the past. And only by keeping it there can I remain in serious contention for major titles.

The positional shot is a tactical ploy. Here, red is holding shot, but precariously. It is vital with his final bowl to protect his position at the back of the head. Otherwise, the jack could easily be driven to score three against him

The draw shot (and variations)

There are a few variations on the draw shot, although they are really tactical variations rather than technical ones. You may want to cover an opponent's bowl that is not lying shot at the moment but might come to be at a later stage (if the jack were disturbed). This is called a positional shot, and while it might be played anywhere in the head it is usually played behind the jack. You play it exactly as a draw shot, except that you substitute the position for the jack as your target, and adjust line and length accordingly.

The rest shot is similar, except that here the path to the jack is obstructed by the bowl lying shot. The shot bowl becomes, in effect, the jack, and the object is to draw right up to it – to rest against it, thereby taking shot. The crucial consideration with this shot is not to fall short. Even quite a firm nudge against the target bowl should still see you in the shot position.

The block shot, another type of draw, is what its name implies. It is an attempt to block your opponent's approach to the head by placing a bowl short, in his path. A block shot just a few feet short of the head is more likely to be effective against an intended draw shot. Far short of the head it is more likely to thwart the drive. In either case, judgment about how and where to block will depend both upon the lie of the bowls and your opponent's intentions, such as you can divine them. It will be obvious, moreover, that a poorly conceived or executed block shot is a completely wasted bowl – just another instance of the premium placed on skill with the draw shot.

Red is holding shot, but there is grave danger that the jack will be trailed to the opposition bowls at the back of the head. An accurate rest shot removes the threat

Target bowls (right) provides
excellent practice for the draw shot

Things look good for red – just so
long as the jack is not driven
towards the ditch. A clever block
shot safeguards the three-shot
advantage

With a rest shot (above) the success
or failure can sometimes be
measured by a hair's breadth

Running shots

The term running shots can be used to describe all shots played with greater than draw weight, but it is conventional to distinguish between the various shots that require only a little more than draw weight, and those that are rather more full-blooded. In this section we will examine the former: the trail, the tap and lie, the wick and the yard on.

The trail

The trail is arguably the most difficult shot in bowls. It involves bowling to the jack with enough extra weight to carry the jack through to another position further back in the head (or even in the ditch). The difficulty in doing this will be obvious. The jack is only $2\frac{1}{2}$ inches in diameter, which makes it a tiny target. Moreover, it is a high-risk shot where getting it nearly right can be worse than missing entirely. If you are trying to trail the jack a few feet up the green (to place it near one or more of your bowls) and instead of hitting it flush succeed only in striking a glancing blow, the jack may go where you least want it to go (in the direction of your opponent's bowls). The shot, therefore, requires pinpoint accuracy, and any shot that demands this should be used sparingly.

You must weigh the potential reward against the potential risk, and convince yourself that under the circumstances the odds favour an attempted trail shot more than they do an alternative. As a rule, the trail shot only becomes a realistic prospect towards the latter stages of an end – commonly as the final shot, where a

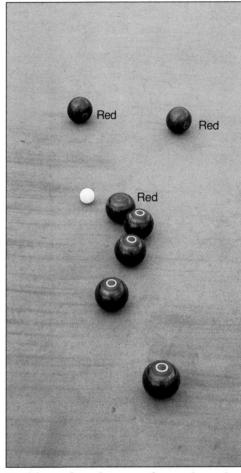

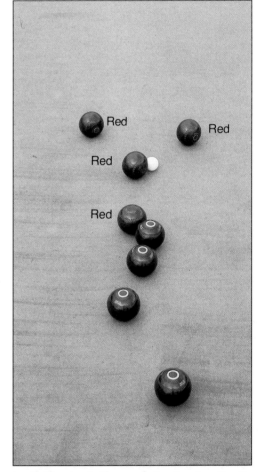

Red has already won the end, and could if he chose try to draw for a second shot. It is better, however, to

trail the jack through to the back of the head for a score of at least three – or as it turns out four

successful trail can make a count.

In playing the trail, you can assume that the jack, when struck, will travel approximately the same distance as the bowl would have travelled had the jack not intervened. In other words, you should imagine yourself drawing to the spot where you want the jack to come to rest. If you take that imaginary draw line back to the mat, you will see that you need a little more weight than you would to draw to the jack, and a little less green, since the bias will be marginally less effective with the increased weight.

The faster the green, the more difficult the trail shot becomes, and in Australia and New Zealand it is largely ignored. Those slick, quick surfaces make it impossible to play so precise and delicate a shot with confidence, and when we went to Australia for the World Championship Triples in 1980 we realized that it was beyond us. We held a team meeting and decided to drop the trail shot from our repertoire for that series.

Tap and lie

The tap and lie shot plays a very large part in the British game, especially outdoors. The object is to replace an existing bowl (usually your opponent's, but not always) with your own. To play it you draw to the object bowl with perhaps two feet extra running. Played perfectly, the tap and lie results in the object ball being 'tapped' gently out of the way, with your bowl 'lying' in the space vacated. The reason this shot figures so prominently in outdoor conditions is

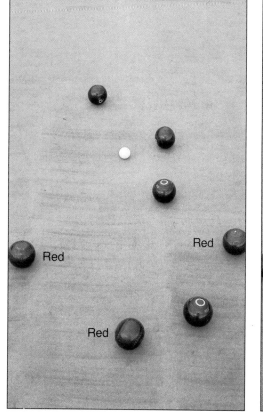

Theoretically, red could steal this end with a perfect draw shot on his final bowl. But a tap and lie shot

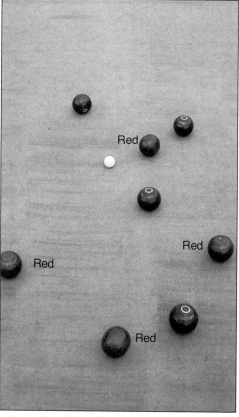

played to the shot bowl allows for a greater margin of error to achieve the same winning result

that it allows a fair margin of error (more than the draw shot, which it tends to replace as the end progresses). Because it is played with a couple of feet extra running it should at least stay the course, and it tends not to matter whether it just barely dislodges the object bowl or knocks it a little further through. Even if you miss it, assuming your weight is about right you are likely to have a bowl well positioned in the head. The worse the conditions, the more attractive the tap and lie shot becomes, and

Scottish bowlers such as Willie McQueen are truly famed for it – he was known as 'the machine' because of the remorseless way he would just tap and lie, tap and lie, either replacing his opponent's bowl or piling up his own score when he was lying shot. As with the trail shot, the tap and lie hardly figures in the Southern Hemisphere, and when the Australians and New Zealanders play outdoors in Britain (as at Aberdeen during the 1984 World Championships) they labour at a disadvantage.

Running shots

The wick

The wick shot is to bowls what the kiss is to snooker – and, like the kiss, it is generally regarded as a fluke, although it can be deliberately played by a good player. It involves bowling at another bowl so as to strike it at a desired angle in order to cannon off it in a particular direction. If the shot bowl is impregnable (by direct attack), then the wick shot may be the only way of reaching it, or reaching the jack. Given the distance involved, the wick is if anything even more difficult to execute than the trail, and it is properly regarded as a rather desperate remedy for a desperate situation. However, in such circumstances, a successfully executed wick shot can transform an end, and even a match.

The yard on

The term yard on implies more precision than this very common shot actually entails. The yard on is similar to the tap and lie, but it is played with rather more running (literally, a yard, rather than the couple of feet associated with the tap and lie). In reality, it is played with anything up to two yards' running, making it an alternative to the heavier drive shots. It is usually employed as a rescue shot, when the head is against you and you want to shift the shot bowl well out of the way. The extra pace cuts down on the bias, which makes it a comparatively direct shot. Again, it favours heavy conditions and is therefore mainly used in Britain.

Red's plight is fairly desperate (above), with no direct route to the jack. A cunningly executed wick shot rescues the situation –

cannoning off his own bowl to the jack and even trailing the jack for good measure, and a possible three

The yard on shot is called for here because red is effectively frozen out of the head. By taking out the

opposition bowl furthest to the right, red slots neatly into shot position

Power shots

Red is up against it here, and with his final bowl he must strike a decisive blow. A full-blooded drive can be a bit of a lottery, but here it has worked wonders, routing the opposition bowls and leaving red with three shots

There are any number of degrees of variation between the yard on shot and the full power drive, but in my opinion it is not particularly helpful to use different names to distinguish between the differing degrees of pace. Whether you are trying to take an opponent's bowl clear of the head, or trail the jack a considerable distance to the ditch, or create mayhem in a head that is horribly against you by sending down a real flyer, you are employing essentially the same shot.

The important thing to remember is that the greater the pace, the less the bias, and while you can never eliminate bias completely, at the upper end of pace the line from mat to target becomes pretty straight. Fashions come and go, and I remember a time when the drive was frowned upon in Britain as being rather ungentlemanly, and there are still those who think that reliance on the drive detracts from the more varied skills of the game. They find it aesthetically displeasing. I personally use the drive shot less than most, but for practical rather than aesthetic reasons. I prefer to pin my colours to the draw shot, in its various guises, and if you can draw consistently well then you have little need for the drive, which is essentially a recovery shot.

The Australians and New Zealanders are very keen on the drive, because their native conditions do not favour the more graduated running shots. Moreover, they tend to drive very hard in order to counter the extreme bias caused by those fast greens. Rob Parrella, for example, has been known to belt the jack straight into the crowd, and if he is not actually a hazard to life and limb he is certainly a hazard to an opponent's bowls, which can shatter under such awesome impact.

The tactics of bowls are relatively straightforward. In every end you have only to build the head in such a way as to make it increasingly difficult for your opponent to gain final advantage, and increasingly likely that you will emerge with one or more shots to your credit. You must, of course, take into account the particular circumstances of the match as it evolves, but in the final analysis you are simply trying to out-bowl your opponent. To do that requires a combination of technical skill and tactical astuteness, and in a contest of equals the latter will almost certainly be decisive. You must learn to read the green accurately, and to use mat and jack imaginatively in order to create and then press home an advantage. Above all, you must become judicious – neither reckless nor timorous – in your choice of shot.

Reading the green

In the preceding chapters there were references to the variability of playing surfaces, mainly in the context of technical adaptation, geographical playing styles and so forth. When it comes to tactics, the matter of reading surfaces astutely and tailoring your game accordingly is of the most critical importance. It is no exaggeration to say that this is an overriding tactical consideration in the game. Skill in this area will not in itself make you a good bowler, but lack of it will make you a loser regardless of your ability to deliver a bowl.

Depending upon the scope of your bowling career you may have to adapt to the differences between outdoor and indoor greens, and possibly between greens 12,000 miles apart – in bowling terms, at least, quite another world. Even if you are one of life's resolute 'homers', you will know that your club green will vary dramatically in the course of a season, sometimes so in the course of a match and even occasionally in the course of a single end. The keenest gardener has no more vested an interest in the state of the ground beneath his feet than has the serious bowler.

Broadly speaking, the condition of outdoor greens in the UK has declined in recent years, noticeably so since I took up the game two decades ago. The reasons for this unhappy state of affairs are not difficult to discern. They are largely connected with money. The many bowling greens that provide one of the amenities of public parks have suffered inescapably as a result of

The greenkeeper is an essential participant in the outdoor game

decreasing staff levels. There are no short cuts to maintaining greens properly, and if those charged with looking after public parks are spread too thinly then the greens will suffer. There may be sound reasons for such economies, but they obviously carry a price.

Club greens too, for the most part, are not as well tended as they used to be. This is not a nostalgic view. It is

simply a recognition of the fact that bowls has always prided itself on being an inexpensive sport (just compare your club fees with those of a comparable golf club!). There was a time when it was possible to combine cheapness with a high level of green maintenance, but those days are long gone and bowlers should face the harsher realities. Most clubs do not employ the services of a full-time greenkeeper (as they once did, in a bygone age of cheap labour costs), and unless they are prepared to pay realistically for such a privilege they never will. You will not get a first-rate green without a first-rate greenkeeper, and the latter are becoming increasingly scarce as the demand for their skills wanes. As a very small child, I remember a club that employed an old greenkeeper who cut the greens with a scythe – with marvellous results. Will we find such skills, such dedication again? And do we deserve to, unless we are prepared to stump up the necessary money to pay for it? Cheap subscriptions are the handmaiden of mediocre greens.

Perversely, there are those who actually relish scrappy greens. They think it is good fun to find a treacherous wet patch or some other gross imperfection that adds an unpredictability to the game. They think, quite rightly, that poor greens reduce the element of skill, and that levelling out the gap between good and bad players is all rather jolly – the rough and ready green encouraging a rough and ready democracy. Such a notion is literally barbaric. Playing snooker on a table covered with rush matting, I might be in with a chance against

Even the most dedicated staff can be powerless in the face of the elements. A sudden deluge in Edinburgh during the 1986 Commonwealth Games simply washed out a day's play at Balgreen

Steve Davis. Bowling on a cabbage patch, he might fancy his arm against me. Surely the point about games of skill is that they should reflect and reward skill as much as possible. That is a prime factor in the rising popularity of indoor greens, with their near-uniform surfaces, and it would in my opinion be a terrible pity if we bowlers were to allow the outdoor game to degenerate because we were not prepared to pay for our pleasure.

Assessing the basic quality of a particular green is not all that difficult, and for the most part you will know it from experience. That is, you will know that your club green is pretty good (smooth, well rolled and cut and therefore consistent) or pretty bad

(the opposite). You will know its peculiarities, such as they are, and you will have learned to take them into account. Even more certain is that you will be aware at any time how the climatic conditions tend to affect the running of the bowls. You do not need much experience to work out the implications of sunny and dry or windy and damp or any other combination. They are pretty well self-evident, in general terms. The skill comes in observing the degree or extent to which any of these factors, or rather these many factors in combination, are affecting a particular green at a particular time, and then adapting your game to suit. That is the skill of reading greens.

Green speed

In bowling parlance, the speed of a green is measured in seconds. It is calculated as the number of seconds it takes a bowl to draw from mat to jack (assumed for the purposes of this calculation to be thirty yards). The faster the green, the longer it will take. In other words, if the green is fast the resistance the bowl encounters on its journey will be low; if it is to pull up by the time it reaches the jack it must be bowled at a comparatively gentle pace, and it will take its time getting there. If the green is slow the resistance is high; the bowl must be delivered with more pace, and that extra pace cuts down the journey time. Hence the seeming paradox that quickness of green equates with slowness of journey time. In the UK, the range of green speeds likely to be encountered is, on average, between ten and twelve seconds. In Australia, and even more so in New Zealand, it is common to find greens running at eighteen seconds and even faster. It is small wonder, therefore, that home advantage in international competitions is even more advantageous than it is in most sports.

Greenkeepers in Australia try to take the guesswork out of reading the speed of their green by publishing a figure for it each day. The intention is helpful, but I do not put much store by it, and certainly in the UK such a policy would probably cause nothing but confusion. That is because so many things can and will alter the speed throughout the course of a day. A sunny day may be interrupted by a sudden shower. Mere cloud cover will slow down a green. Either a tailwind or a headwind will make non-

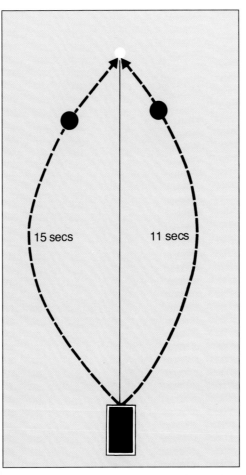

Green speed may vary significantly between forehand and backhand. The wide hand is the faster side, the narrow the slower

sense of a predicted speed. Even if nothing untoward occurs during the course of a lovely English summer day, the speed will vary, from comparatively slow early on while dew

lies on the grass, to maximum speed through the heat of the afternoon, then slowing down again as the sun begins to sink and the cooler night air arrives.

You must get into the habit of observing even the tiniest changes in green speed during the course of play, so that you can make the necessary adjustments. If you tend to be just a few minutes – a single end – ahead of your opponent in assessing these changes, consider what an advantage this gives you. Furthermore, do not fall into the easy trap of thinking that this or that climatic change will necessarily have predictable results. Normally they will have, but not always, and it is what is actually happening to the green that you must respond to, not what you think should be happening. For example, I have played on greens with a lot of water lying on them that were relatively fast – the bowl skimming along on a film of water. Then the sun has come out and dried up that superficial water quickly. The result? A much slower green, because the sun has been drawing the deeper damp out of the ground making the green sodden where earlier it had been slick.

The reason that it is critical to gauge the speed of the green is twofold. It is essential to judging pace, obviously, but it is just as essential to estimating bias. The faster the green, the greater the arc from mat to jack. On the slowest of greens, the curve will be modest. On the fastest, it will be sweeping – in New Zealand, the bowl almost makes a ninety-degree turn as it rolls to a halt.

The hotter and drier it is, the faster the green speed (above, Tony Allcock watching his opponent George Souza Jnr. of Hong Kong). Rain slows the pace considerably (right, the Australians in green having to cope with 'foreign' conditions during the 1986 Commonwealth Games at Edinburgh)

Crosswinds

While light breezes have little discernible effect on a bowl, driving wind is a serious hazard and very blustery conditions are any bowler's nightmare. Bowling into the teeth of a gale, or with a strong tailwind, makes a mockery of any expectations about green speed, and will necessitate more or less drastic alterations to your weight of shot to achieve any particular result. By the law of averages, however, at least some degree of crosswind is much more likely to plague you.

A crosswind will have the predictable effect of either accentuating or countering the bowl's bias, by applying force in the direction it is blowing. If it is blowing from left to right, it will narrow the forehand played by a right-hander, and widen the backhand. It is often said that under such circumstances it is safer to play the narrower hand, and all other things being equal that is sound policy. It is not, however, to be taken as a golden rule, because other factors (like a favourable and unfavourable side of

the rink) can intervene. What can be taken as a rule is this: in windy conditions, stick to the hand that is showing the more consistent effect of the wind. This will usually be the narrow hand.

Quite apart from the sartorial problem of keeping your hat on, playing in high winds is awkward. Head or tailwinds invalidate any expectations of green speeds, while a crosswind will either accentuate or diminish the effects of bias

The human effect

It is easy to see why the ditch rinks, with all the wear and tear they get when they are not 'in use', tend to run faster than their neighbours

The climate is not alone in affecting the running. On any given rink, one side may be running as much as a few seconds faster than the other because of human intervention. Where a green has been artificially watered, one part may have received more water than its neighbour, and if those two adjacent areas lie within the same rink there will be an effect. If during the course of a day one side of a rink receives significantly more play than the other, it will become faster. As the strings are moved, in order to ensure uniform wear on the green as a whole over a period, at any given time you are likely to find one side more worn, and therefore faster, than the other. This is particularly noticeable around the sides of the green. Ditch rinks tend to run faster because of all the wear and tear they get when the green is switched at right angles.

To a greater or lesser extent, depending upon how well the green has been tended, tracking will occur in the course of a game, and certainly in the course of a day. This tracking – a flattening of the grass along the principal line or lines of play – will be more pronounced if the grass has not been closely cut, or regularly scarified. The area that is tracking becomes quicker than the rest of the green. In extreme cases, it will result in the formation of a groove or grooves between mat and jack, and this will have a bearing on the tactical use of mat and jack – especially the mat. You may want to force your opponent literally out of the groove.

I hope it will be becoming increasingly clear why I feel as strongly as I

do about sticking to one set of bowls. You have only two trial ends before a match. That gives you a maximum of eight bowls (down to four, if you are playing fours) in which to figure out how the rink is playing. In this section I have only touched on the main variables and in the most general terms, yet even so it is a fair amount to have to contend with. You will judge the matter for yourself, but as far as I am concerned I will not willingly make it any more complex than it is, and to throw different bowls into the equation is to add to the complexity.

One would be forgiven for thinking that the answer to a bowler's prayers

would be a synthetic green, and indeed several years ago some interesting prototypes appeared on the scene. They ran fast and true, and it was hoped that easier maintenance would make them cheaper in the long run. The trouble with them was that they were bedevilled by drainage problems, and they were more than normally unpredictable. In consequence they no longer seem to be a pointer to the future. The outdoor game will be played on grass for the foreseeable future, with all the pleasure, the frustration, and the sheer variety that entails.

Indoor greens

Indoor bowls is growing rapidly in popularity and will continue to do so. It enables year-round play, and indoor greens offer conditions that are, if not uniform, at least not subject to anything like the unpredictability of those outdoors. Free from wind, rain and the vagaries (or absence) of green-keeping skills, indoor greens offer the skilled player an excellent platform for displaying his skills, and the not-so-skilled player a perfect environment for improving his technique. The fact that indoor greens are almost always good, however, does not mean that you can ignore the discipline of reading them.

The carpet for a modern indoor green is laid on a concrete base called a screed, and because no two screeds are quite identical, so no two indoor greens will play identically. Indoor greens are always fast (by outdoor UK standards), but some are faster than others, and therefore take more bias. These differences between greens are certainly minor compared to what is encountered outdoors, but they exist, and, because indoor conditions encourage bowling of a higher standard, understanding even very subtle peculiarities of the green can be the difference between winning and losing. Older indoor greens are often laid on a wooden base. Experienced players are rightly wary of such greens, because in time the wooden boards are prone to warping or shrinking. This will play havoc with a smooth surface, so if you have any choice in the matter always opt for the newer, concrete-based green.

Despite being sheltered from the elements, indoor greens are affected

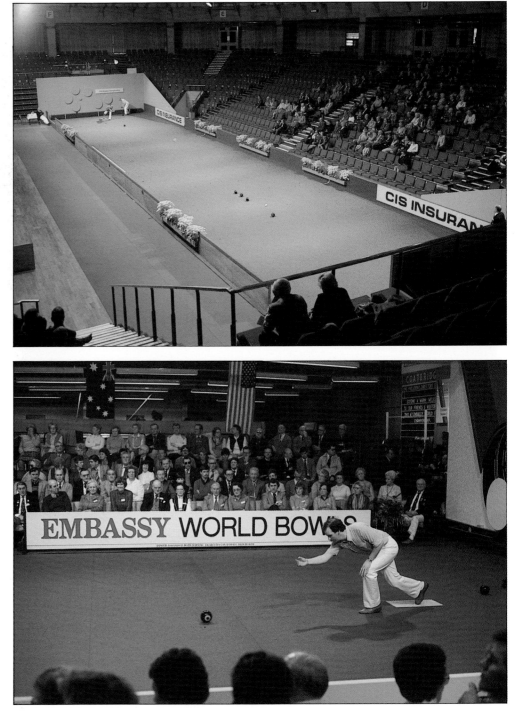

Willie Wood asks Bob Crawshaw to
confirm the score in the 1986
Superbowl tournament at
Manchester. The growth in the
indoor game and the success of TV
bowls have gone hand in hand

by climatic conditions. On a frosty morning, for example, they tend to run a little faster than normal, and on a muggy day they run slower. I am not entirely certain of the scientific explanation for these phenomena, but they are well known to be the case. Remember, as with bowling outdoors, not to assume that you know in advance the way the green will behave, even if you are playing on home ground. Use your trial bowls to assess the actual situation at the moment. It is essential on trial ends to use the maximum number of bowls permitted you.

The portable TV rink (left), in action here at Preston Guild Hall, is used for many televised tournaments. It is assembled from 120 laser-levelled segments, and has a crumb rubber underlay and a woollen carpet surface. It takes seven hours to construct, two hours to dismantle

Jim Baker (left) on his way to victory in the World Indoor Singles Championship at Coatbridge in 1984. The near-perfect playing conditions on such a rink go as close as possible to ensuring the triumph of bowling skill

Celebrity bowls (right) is an enjoyable aspect of the game – from the left, football managers Tommy Docherty and Ron Atkinson, cricketers Ian Botham and Bob Willis

Use of mat and jack

The mat and the jack can be looked at in two ways. Viewed simply, they are, respectively, the thing you stand on to deliver your bowl and the target towards which play is directed. Those are their irreducible functions, but it would pay you to see them in another light as well. Used with skill and cunning, the mat and jack, individually and together, play an important tactical role in the game.

The laws of bowls are designed to add such a tactical dimension. At the beginning of a game, the mat must be placed specifically – centred in the rink and with the front edge six feet from the ditch. Each end thereafter, the player to bowl first has the right to advance the mat (always centred) anywhere up the rink to a point no less than twenty seven yards from the front ditch. The mat remains where it is placed for the entire end.

The jack is cast from the usual bowling position on the mat, and must come to rest within the confines of the rink, no less than twenty five yards from the front of the mat (in the British Isles). If it comes to rest within two yards of the front ditch (a full-length jack) it is brought back to the two-yard mark and centred (as it is wherever it comes to rest). The important implication of this is that the jack can only be successfully delivered from the extreme forward mat position if it is a full-length jack. Less than that, and it is not twenty five yards from the mat.

These laws place a significant premium on being able to throw the jack with more than some accuracy. Keeping it within the side confines of the

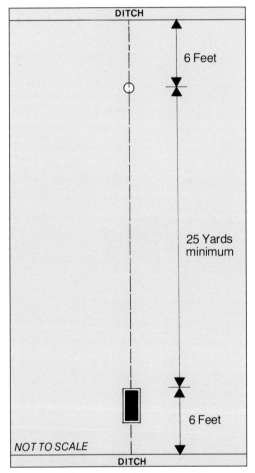

At the beginning of a game, the mat is centred in the rink, with the leading edge six feet from the ditch. The jack, having been cast no less than twenty five yards from the front of the mat (in the British Isles), is in turn centred. For most recent IBB amendment, see Laws of the Game, The Green, pages 125–26

rink is not unduly difficult – mercifully, since there is nothing more embarrassing than watching a poorly delivered jack wander into an adjoining rink. Gauging length accurately demands skill and experience, and it is critical to effective use of the mat. If, for example, you choose to take the mat as far up the rink as the laws permit (as I frequently do), you must have confidence that you can deliver the jack to a full length and short of the ditch. Wherever you position the mat, if you decide to deliver a short jack, you must do so confident of not falling short of the twenty five-yard mark.

When it comes to delivering the jack, the most important point to bear in mind is that it is not biased, so it will travel from the mat in a straight line. Stand on the mat as you would for a draw shot, with your feet facing the line – straight down the middle of the rink. Opinions vary as to how you should hold the jack. David Bryant, who prefers the claw grip in any case, argues that it is best to deliver the jack from the fingertips. He reckons that delivering it from the palm (the cradle grip) increases the risk of sending the jack off centre. From my experience, this is not so. I use my normal cradle grip, and consider that delivering the jack from the fingers runs the risk of putting unintentional spin on it, thereby getting deviation. Given this disagreement, you would be advised to please yourself, and it is likely that your choice will be determined by whether you favour the claw or the cradle grip.

Another point of minor controversy is whether or not to hold a

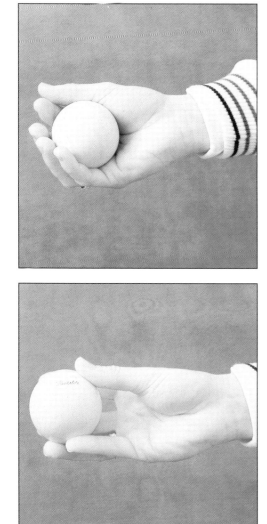

Some players prefer to deliver the jack from the palm of the hand (top), others from the fingertips (above). Tony Allcock (right) instructs the marker to move the jack to the right, in order to centre it

Use of mat and jack

bowl in one hand while delivering the jack with the other. Those who do so believe that they more easily retain the feeling of length after bowling the jack if they simply have to transfer the bowl from hand to hand. They think that reaching down to pick up a bowl interferes with the continuity. They may well be right, but I do not follow their example. I want nothing, except possibly a cloth, in my left hand when I am bowling. If you feel more comfortable holding a bowl, by all means do so, but avoid the common mistake of holding it away from the body while delivering the jack. It will affect your balance.

There is endless debate about whether you should take the jack if you win the toss at the beginning of the game. Assuming that you can deliver the jack more or less on target, it might seem obvious that you would choose to take the opportunity to take that initiative, in the same way that tennis players routinely elect to serve. It is not as simple with bowls, however, because having the final bowl is also an advantage, and it is therefore a question of choosing between rival attractions.

I look at it this way. Having the last bowl is a *definite* advantage. Determining the position of the jack is a *notional* advantage, and only sometimes is that notional, or theoretical, advantage of practical importance. When it is, it governs your choice. The important thing, therefore, is to judge whether or not the particular circumstances justify waiving the last bowl for the first jack.

Many factors come to bear on this, and the situation is rather different

Tony Allcock signals the marker after delivering the jack. 'Move it to the left. That's it.' The jack is always centred, regardless of length

for singles as opposed to team play. In singles, you get to deliver eight trial bowls, which should enable you to get a fair idea of the way the green is running on both hands. This means that by taking the jack you may be in a position to exploit any peculiarities of the green from the outset. If you bowl your first bowl close to the jack you are likely to be in the driving seat for that end, and there is nothing better than getting off to a flying start. If you are playing fours, by contrast, you (as lead) have only four trial bowls, and it is therefore much less likely that you will have been able to discern the advantages of playing to a particular length. Having the final

bowl (as skip), provides you with a good chance of converting the head, and all things being equal that would be the natural choice.

So far so good, but the complexities can mount. Suppose you know that your opponent (or opponents) have a preference for short jacks. Would it not be a good idea to unsettle them by immediately forcing them to play to a full-length jack? Or suppose you (or your team) feel more confident with a short jack. Why not capitalize at once on your luck in winning the toss? And so it goes on. You may have a preconceived game play that dictates taking the first jack if offered. You may just feel that you are beginning the game 'hot', and that by drawing close to the jack on the first shot you will gain a psychological advantage. Or you may be feeling 'cold', in which case...

Tony Allcock delivering the jack. The action is identical to his bowling action, the only difference being that he aims directly at his chosen target spot because the jack is unbiased

Use of mat and jack

Finally, there is the question of what you do if the game goes to an extra end. There is another toss for the jack, and the mat is fixed as at the beginning of the game. To take the jack or not? The same range of considerations apply, but with a difference. At this advanced point you know the strengths and weaknesses (on the day) of both teams. You will have observed that your opponents have been having greater success with one length than another, and similarly for yourselves. You will know that your lead has been drawing more consistently than theirs, or vice versa. And you will know that you, as skip, are on song or off key when it comes to the final bowl. However, unless there are compelling reasons for controlling the jack under these circumstances, my feeling is that holding final bowl is too good an opportunity to decline.

As to the tactical positioning of the jack itself (ignoring for the moment the related tactical use of the mat), I personally favour the full-length jack. There are several reasons for this. First, if your opposition is inexperienced, or an unknown quantity, you might as well assume until proven otherwise that setting up a head near the ditch will cause them more problems than it causes you. Inexperienced bowlers tend to be afraid of running into the ditch, and they are therefore liable to bowl short. Second, only by bowling a full-length jack can you know exactly where it is going to be. Anything short of a full length, and you will be playing the jack where it comes to rest. But if you bowl it full length – anywhere within

two yards of the ditch – you know it will be centred on the two-yard marker. This naturally assumes that you can gauge the length of the jack to within two yards, and with occasional lapses I can. Third, establishing the head near the ditch encourages the shots at the more subtle draw and rest end of the spectrum, at the expense of the heavy drives. That is where my main strengths lie, so I naturally take what steps I can to dictate that type of play.

In practice, you cannot consider the length of jack in isolation from the positioning of the mat. Some players

Charles McGhee of Wales centres a full-length jack – on the marker two yards short of the ditch

move the mat around more than others, and in that sense I would be classified as a mat mover. There are two fundamental reasons for moving the mat, although they are really opposite sides of the same coin – the coin that is the common currency of all tactical games. You move the mat either to position it to your own playing advantage, or to position it to your opponent's disadvantage – both, if you are lucky. You might want to move the mat up or down the green if the green is tracking and you are having difficulty in finding a line. There may be other imperfections in the green's surface that you want to avoid. There can be any number of reasons why you might fancy moving the mat for the sake of your own shot playing.

Making things as easy as possible for yourself is equalled, perhaps outweighed, by the attraction of making them as difficult as possible for the other fellow. He (or they) may be bowling well to a certain length, and badly to another. You will want to move the mat accordingly. A mat position that is good for you may be even better for your opponent, in which case you have more to gain than lose by chancing a different position. Conversely, a mat position that poses difficulties for you may be proving utterly horrific for him (as witness, the scoreboard), in which case you will want to persevere with it. He may find frequent mat changes unsettling in themselves, and if you sense that (or know it from experience) you will want to capitalize on his lack of flexibility. David Ward, a current England skip, has become an extreme exponent of this technique. He has great faith in his team's ability to bowl to any length. Given this versatility, he deploys the mat to the maximum in order to keep his opponents from settling. He sometimes instructs his lead to move the mat at every opportunity – regardless of whether or not he is on a winning length.

I fall some way short of such aggressive use of the mat, but I do consider it a formidable weapon to

Charles McGhee uses the full width of the mat to play the backhand

have at my disposal. I tend to move it up the green for any combination of the reasons outlined, and for another one as well. While I like to bowl to a full-length jack, I also prefer a short jack. The shorter the distance between mat and jack, the greater the emphasis on the sort of touch shots that are the cornerstone of my game. To achieve that combination of circumstances, I am inclined to take the mat towards the front peg.

Imaginative use of the mat is not restricted to the tactical considerations of moving it up or down the rink. Whatever the position of the

mat, you may if you wish deliver off the front or the back of it, or off either side. Moving forward or backward on the mat will in theory provide an automatic corrective if you find yourself bowling consistently a foot or so short or long, but in my view it is a rather desperate measure. Only by bowling from the same position on the mat can you remain confident of picking out the line, and it really is an admission of defeat to resign yourself to unmanageable length. Moving to the back of the mat in particular carries a hazard, because it means you will be grounding the bowl perilously near the front edge.

Using either the inside or outside of the mat is another matter, and while I rarely do so myself it is not a ploy to be discounted out of hand. If an intervening bowl has made the line to the jack difficult or impossible, shifting to one side or the other may well open up a path. During the Bournemouth Open tournament a few years ago, I watched in astonishment as a young skip from Devon used this tactic to most telling effect. At a critical point in a match he found himself comprehensively blocked by an opposition bowl. Taking advantage of his considerable height (well over six feet), he planted his left foot towards the side of the mat, stepped fully three feet to the right and nonchalantly delivered a perfect forehand past the blocker and sweetly into the head. The fact that this incident impressed itself so vividly on my memory suggests that it was an extreme example of the technique, but bear in mind that it is at your disposal in an emergency.

Choice of shot

This is an open-ended subject because the game allows for an infinite number of specific situations, and choice of shot must always come down to selecting the option that best suits any particular circumstance. As the head begins to build it takes on its unique shape, a shape that you have never seen exactly reproduced before and will never see exactly reproduced again. Therefore, you are forced to keep solving one-off problems. And with each bowl, the situation changes again, always in a novel manner. Moreover, the state of the head as you observe it is never the only consideration as you weigh up your choice of shot. You will necessarily be taking into account the condition of the green as it relates to your options, your particular bowling strengths and weaknesses, what you consider to be your opponent's strengths and weaknesses, your confidence at the moment (and your assessment of your opponent's), the potential profit if a particular shot is successful, and loss if it is not, and the state of the game as a whole – near the beginning or end, with you well ahead or behind or level pegging. This is not an exhaustive list of the things that have a bearing on choice of shot, but it gives an indication of the complexities involved. If you play to be a hundred, you will never get to the bottom of it, but then that is why the game is infinitely challenging.

Having said that, it is by no means futile to discuss choice of shot, or for you as a bowler to think long and hard about it while away from the heat of battle. There are sound general principles that apply, and, while no two situations are absolutely identical, a thorough understanding of those principles is an essential part of your tactical equipment.

The first requisite for shot selection is an accurate picture of the existing situation. David Bryant wants to be sure that he has heard the marker aright, during the 1985 Gateway Masters against Dennis Katunarich

George Souza Jnr. of Hong Kong
works out his strategy, while his
opponent Tony Allcock looks on
reflectively – already thinking
ahead to his own next shot, perhaps

Choice of shot

In the next chapter I will discuss some of the peculiarities of singles and team play, and attempt to analyse the individual roles in a team. The distinctions involved are obviously important when it comes to shot selection, but for the moment either ignore them or assume knowledge of them. Some of the principles of shot selection are universal in their application, while others are more relevant to skips than leads or the reverse. It should be apparent from the context of the examples where they most apply, and in any event you must keep in mind that they are general principles, and make sense in particular circumstances only when viewed in the light of those circumstances. You should aim to be the master of theory, not its slave.

In bowls, as in snooker, tennis and presumably every other ball game, great use is made of the phrase 'percentage shot'. Television commentators are forever saying that this or that competitor is 'playing the percentages', or is adopting a high risk strategy (by definition, against the percentages). It can be made to appear rather cold, like an exercise in accountancy, and who wants to adopt such a calculating approach to a game? It is easy to caricature the percentage player as methodical and dull, timorous even, and to identify with those freer spirits who throw caution to the winds. In this view, the inescapable fact that the so-called percentage players tend to win more than they lose is just another maddening reflection on the injustice of life.

This is badly to misrepresent percentage play, indeed to misunder-

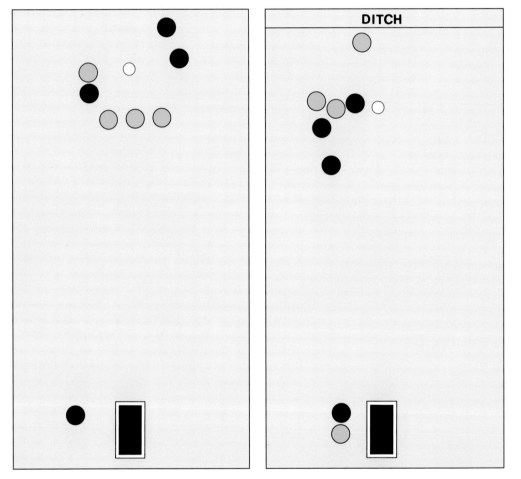

The best chance for black is to wick off his own bowl, which will effectively dismiss the shot bowl and slice the jack for a possible four

Black should attempt to trail the jack around the shot bowl to reduce its vulnerability. Otherwise, green would have the option of driving the jack to the ditch to gain shot — and it would be virtually impossible for black to get the furthest back bowl at this stage

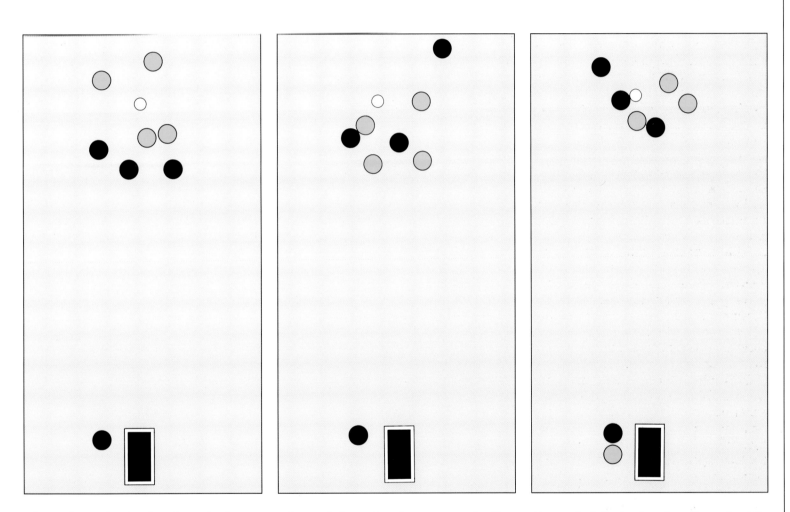

The only realistic shot here is the draw, because black has effectively blocked the shots requiring weight. A weighted bowl would have to gain a perfect result to advance a bowl to the shot position. Some bowlers might gamble on a drive, but the odds would be against them. The draw shot here could be executed on either hand, drawing around the front bowls

The jack here has been moved off centre. The best shot for black would be the yard on played on the forehand between the two green bowls, playing the black through to the jack

Green holds the last bowl, and will most certainly attempt to move the shot bowl, springing the jack towards his own bowls. Black should try to place his final bowl with the two green bowls

Choice of shot

stand what it is and why it must underpin the tactics of any successful competitor at any level of any game. Percentage play is not in itself either monotonous or exciting, cautious or courageous, the tactic of the dour spoiler or the flamboyant attacker. It is simply the practical application of sober thought in a competitive situation. It begins with a realistic appraisal of the available courses of action at any given moment, and then goes on to assess the pros and cons of each. These pros and cons are usually pretty straightforward. If I choose shot A, how likely am I to succeed with it? If I do succeed, what do I gain? If I fail, what am I likely to lose? Under the circumstances, does the prospect of gain outweigh the risk of loss? Taking all in all, is shot A a good gamble, bearing in mind that any shot is a gamble? Taking the analysis further, is shot A a better gamble than shot B or C? Is it, in fact, the best gamble available to me? If so, it is the percentage shot. It is the percentage shot whether I relish it or not, for it may be no more than the best of a bad bunch, and it was the percentage shot even if I go on to play it and miss it. The percentage shot is neither more nor less than that, and to choose it is no guarantee of success. Sometimes you will succeed better, perhaps dramatically so, by ignoring it, but you will never be a good player if you fail to see the relevance of such calculations. To choose an example from a closely related game, Jimmy White has just as keen an appreciation of percentage play as Steve Davis.

Beyond that, it is impossible to define the percentage shot in a way

Noel Burrows may look as though he is telling a fishing tale, but he just wants to make absolutely sure that the critical distance in the head is as he thinks it is

George Turley applauds a shot by John Bell during a triples match against Western Samoa (1984 World Championships). Team play can ease the strain of shot selection because there is advice readily on tap, but of course you still have to get it right — and play it right

Choice of shot

that is applicable to various individuals at various times. A percentage shot for me, for instance, might represent a hopeful long shot for you. Or a percentage shot for me on one occasion might not be on another (a change in the conditions, my form, my mood, the state of the match, and so on). Whatever the percentage shot may happen to be, however, it is imperative that you look for it, and recognize it when you see it. Only then can you make an intelligent judgment about taking a true risk – accepting the challenge of a shot that is against the percentages, but one that you feel is the right choice nevertheless. All good players do

that, some with less reluctance than others, but they do not do so blind to the possible consequences. You will have to go for broke often enough in bowls without looking around for chancy shots just because you get a kick out of pulling them off.

There is no substitute for experi-

The correct choice of shot, and then executing it, separates winners from losers. Here, a prone Wynne Richards and England team-mates watch hawk-like as skip David Ward's final bowl enters the head at Ayr. It missed – just – leaving Wales victorious

ence when it comes to shot selection, but there are a few guidelines that are generally applicable. A golden rule is to try not to bowl jack high and to the side. Just behind or just in front of the jack is a good place to be, but a foot or so to the side is always vulnerable. Such a bowl presents a perfect target for a rest shot, and because it is jack high it is extremely unlikely to come into the reckoning if the jack is trailed.

Having used your trial ends to advantage, you will know if the green is two paced. If it is, try where possible to bowl on the side of the green that better suits you – forehand in one direction, backhand in the other.

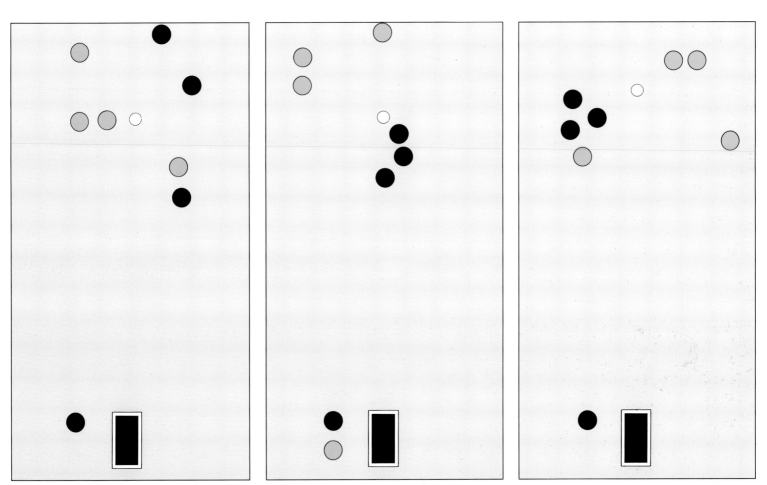

Black has several options. He can attempt a tap and lie against green's shot bowl, or with a similar backhand shot split green's two bowls and in doing so move the jack sideways towards his own bowl. Alternatively, he could trail the jack for three shots. In reality, as long as he bowls with sufficient weight, one of these three results is very likely to occur

Black has to make a clear decision here, based on what he thinks green will attempt with his final bowl. He can place a back bowl to cover the trail, or he can place a side bowl to prevent a count of three, should green play a yard on shot on the forehand to force black's shot bowl on to the jack, thereby sending it towards his own bowls

Black could of course draw to the jack, but he has a better alternative. If he drives and splits green's shot bowl and its neighbour, he may leave himself with a full house

Choice of shot

Obviously it will not always be possible to follow that advice as the head takes shape, but it is a sound policy because it enables you to settle into a rhythm of line and length. How much more difficult that is if you have to take note of whether you are playing on the fast or slow side of the green shot by shot.

Be chary of using running or drive shots early on in a game. You should be striving for line and length, and the latter is the more difficult to get. Get into the drawing groove as quickly as you can, so that you can adjust gradually as the green quickens during the first few ends (as it tends to do, particularly outdoors). Failure to do this can be a costly embarrassment. Suppose, as skip, that you have been relying on take-out shots for the first few ends, and then all of a sudden the jack has been knocked into the open. All you have to do is draw to within a reasonable distance, but how are you going to manage that if you can only guess at the draw weight? You might have a huge margin of error for the shot – several feet – and *still* miss! You lose touch with the pace of the green at your peril.

Get into the habit of keeping the game tight. That is not to suggest negative play, but it is clearly foolish to accrue a few shots' advantage over several ends and then squander them all with a sudden rush of blood to the head. If you do get off to a flying start then of course press home your advantage ruthlessly, but work on the assumption that it is by winning the majority of the close ends that you will win the majority of your games. If

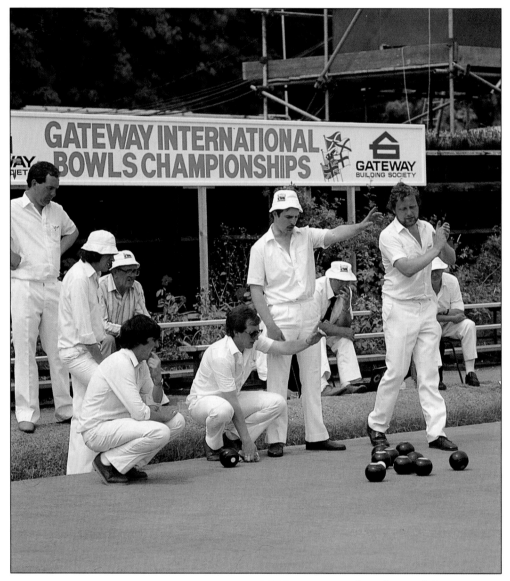

With as many bowls as this surrounding the jack, choosing the correct line and, even more so, the correct weight can make the difference between being on the right or wrong side of a big score

A critical shot during the Ireland v Wales match in the 1983 Home Internationals. When you get it as right as this, no one leaves you in any doubt

Choice of shot

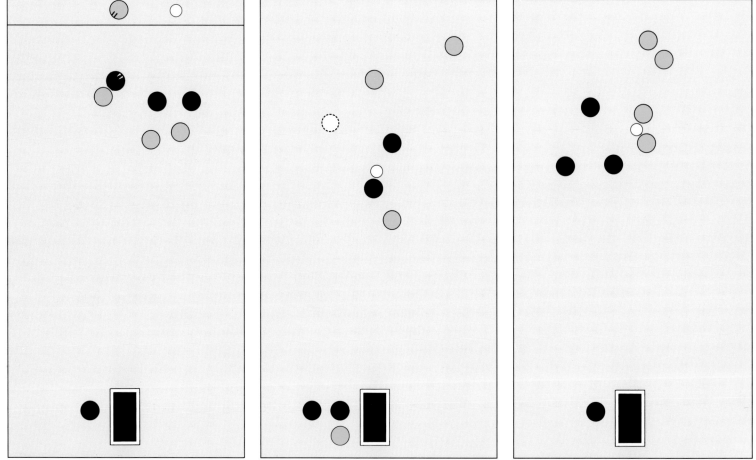

Green has ditched the jack and is holding shot with his toucher. Black is fortunate to have a really good chance of turning the tables with his last bowl. All he has to do is drive on the backhand to the green bowl resting against his own toucher. Because of the favourable angle, his toucher has a very good chance of going into shot position, so long as the shot is played with ditch weight

Black holds two shots, and his only real worry is that green will, with his final bowl, hit the shot bowl and spring the jack towards the back of the head and to his own two back bowls. However, if green does that the jack will cannon off black's own bowl, in the direction of the position indicated. That is where black should put his final bowl

Black needs to tackle a tricky draw shot here, sometimes called 'the draw to reach'. What he must do is use draw weight or a little more to tap the front of green's two counting bowls. This will spring the jack towards black's own bowls and result in a possible three. With this shot, it is obviously imperative not to be under strength

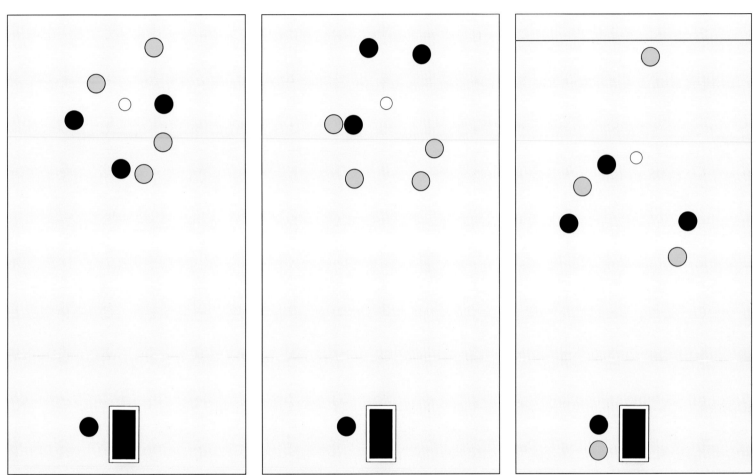

Black's best shot here is the tap and lie on green's shot bowl, for a possible count of three

Black has a good chance of converting his one-shot advantage to four. What he should do is play on the forehand a tap and lie shot against his own shot bowl. This should remove green's nearest bowl. Depending upon the weight used, there is a good chance that the jack will be moved, but that should do no harm to black's winning position

Assume that the score is 20–19 in black's favour. He has a problem. He could play his final shot to the jack, or thereabouts, and hope for the best. Or he could try to get the furthest back bowl. The trouble is, green's back bowl is an excellent one, and black would have great difficulty in beating it. Green will therefore have a good chance of driving the jack to the ditch for two shots and the game. The best thing black can do is trail the jack to a less vulnerable position

Choice of shot

you have a mind to attempt risky shots – shots that are well against the percentages, but could if successful provide a handsome reward – go for them fairly early on. If they come off, your opponent may become demoralized and thereafter easy prey. If they do not, you should have plenty of time to recover.

This is only a very general rule of thumb, and its applicability will vary between singles and team play. In fours, for example, if you are half a dozen shots in front with as many ends to play, it is your opponents who have to take chances, not you. Ignore the temptations of a shot that might pay handsomely if you succeed where it might give your opponents similar reward if you fail – even if the shot itself is relatively easy. It is *not*, under those circumstances, the percentage shot, because the consequences of failure far outweigh any possible gain. Choose the safest shot you can find. Do anything rather than risk letting your opponents back into a game that they have effectively lost by this point.

Somewhat similar circumstances in singles play might suggest a different course of action. If you were leading 17–9, and you had a reasonable chance of gaining a full house, with a two- or three-shot deficit facing you if you should botch the shot, you might well take it on. If you succeed you end the match at a stroke (and with a satisfying flourish), whereas if you fail you are still comfortably in front.

The general point about keeping the game tight has a further application. You start off every end intent on winning it, but, as and when an end

All eyes are fixed on the approaching bowl, as Botswana play Zambia in the 1984 World Championships at Aberdeen. At critical points in a game, it is essential to resist any sudden rush of blood to the head

David Bryant (opposite) is not only a revered bowler, he is one of the game's most penetrating thinkers. No one gives more careful consideration to shot selection – weighing up the rewards of a successful outcome against the penalty of failure

Choice of shot

begins to go against you, you must respond to that evolving situation. You will frequently reach a point at which the end must be considered lost. In the realms of pure theory, mixed with a liberal dash of fantasy, no end is utterly beyond redemption by the saving grace of one miraculous shot, but you would be ill-advised to bank on miracles. How should you set about fighting a rearguard action? I follow a pretty firm rule on this matter. I decline any shot that will, if it fails, leave me even worse off than I was already. Suppose my opponent is lying two and I hold the last bowl. If there is an improbable shot available which will, if I happen to make it, give me shot, or reduce the deficit to one, then I will attempt it – but only if that shot carries no risk of increasing my deficit. I will accept my loss of two, rather than play a shot that might result in my losing four. Even that rule is not hard and fast. It can hardly apply if that two-shot margin is enough to give my opponent the match. Then I have nothing to lose by going for a miraculous winner.

Miracles do happen, and in dire circumstances I have had my share. During the 1986 Gloucestershire County Singles Championship, I found myself on the brink of elimination during the preliminary round. The score was 20-all, and with his last bowl my opponent was a little fortunate to leave himself with a full house. I looked at the position of the four bowls lying against me in the head, and then back down the green, and I despaired. There was no way through. The draw was blocked, the yard on was blocked, everything was

Phil Skoglund (New Zealand) and Tony Allcock take a close look at two bowls contesting the shot position, during the finals of the 1986 World Indoor Singles Championship. This was the first of Tony's successive triumphs in the competition

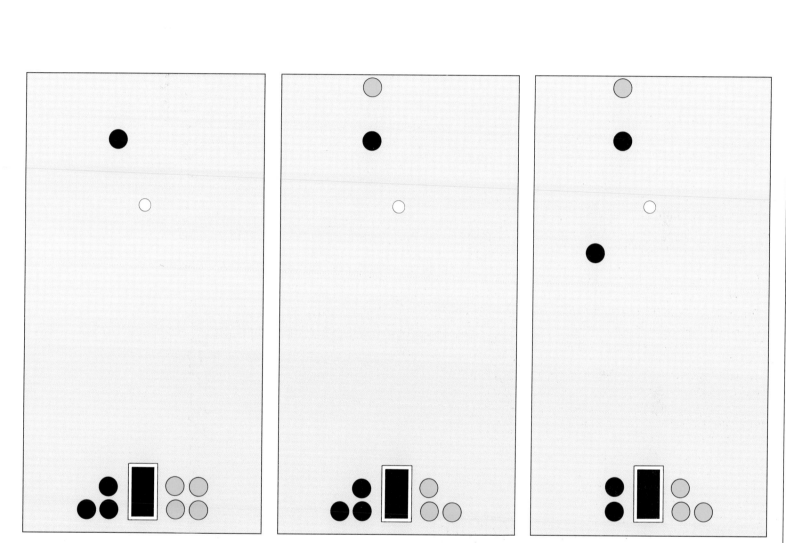

To illustrate the way an end can develop, Tony has selected a particular end that he actually played in the course of the National Indoor Singles Championship area semi-finals in 1987. The score was 20-all, so Tony and his opponent both needed one for the match

'My opponent opened with a draw on the backhand which went some eighteen inches beyond the jack'

'My backhand opening bowl was over-bowled as well, coming to rest a good yard behind the jack'

'My opponent stayed on the backhand, but over-corrected his weight, falling about eighteen inches short of the jack. Unintentionally, he has forced me on to the forehand. That is a real problem because this carpet has a notorious patch that prevents the forehand (in that direction) from bending properly and the bowl just runs straight'

Continued on page 84

Choice of shot

blocked, and I trudged down to the mat resigned to defeat. When I got there I realized that I had become so dejected by the hopelessness of it all that I had not even formed a plan. I had no shot in mind. Now I have not enjoyed the success I have in bowls by playing shots aimlessly, and I immediately pulled myself together. I walked back up the green and studied the head all over again, determined not to return to the mat until I had a plan of action. Sure enough, there was a possible shot, improbable admittedly, but still possible. What I had to do was pick up a short bowl of mine and run it three yards up the green on to the shot bowl, which would move the jack and cannon into the second shot bowl. With the jack dislodged and those two shot bowls split, I would be snugly lying shot. Nothing to it, really – I should say the odds were no more than 100–1 against! In recognition of this reality, most of the spectators were heading for the clubhouse bar.

I returned to the mat in a positive frame of mind (there is no point in attempting any shot, however implausible, in a tentative manner), and played the shot. It came off as though the four bowls and the jack were on strings. Having won the match with that desperate shot, I went on eventually to win the championship. It is not a shot I am ever likely to repeat (let alone succeed with), but if there is a moral to the story it is this: if defeat is staring you in the face, you must commit yourself to some positive course of action, however much the odds are stacked against you. I doubt if I shall ever rescue myself from a worse plight on a bowling green, but I did so on that one important occasion and I did so only because I refused to give in to despair.

The fruits of victory – Tony Allcock with a few reminders of success to date

You should be clear in your mind what you intend to do before stepping on to the mat. Once there, all your energies should be concentrated on executing the shot selected

Choice of shot

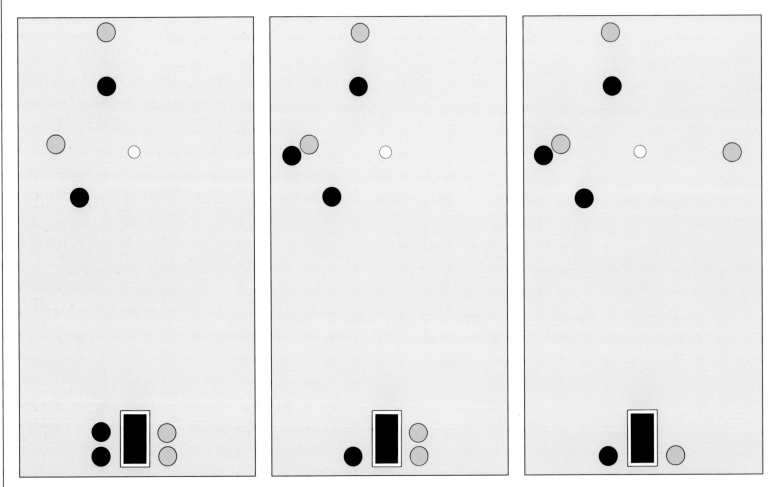

'I played the forehand draw, this time with correct weight, but too narrow as I over-compensated for the tricky patch on the carpet'

'My opponent, again trying to draw on the backhand, succeeded only in falling just outside my jack high bowl'

'My situation was looking grim. There were two shots against me and there was no realistic way of taking those two bowls out. I simply had to draw to that invitingly open jack – which neither of us had succeeded in doing to date. All I had to do was get that forehand line right, and keep the weight I had achieved with my second bowl. To my chagrin, this time I caught the holding piece of carpet and ended up well wide of the jack, and only second shot'

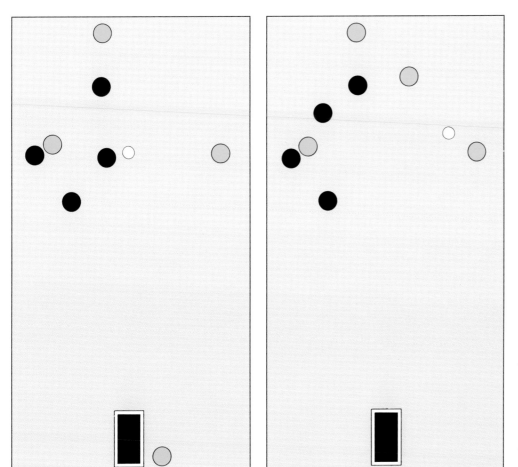

more confident with. Also, the margin of error was considerable. If I played a yard on and came inside the shot bowl, I would trail the jack to my own back bowl (maybe). Against this was the need to avoid my opponent's front bowl, which meant I needed sufficient weight to get inside it and stay on line. (d) The most obvious of all, in theory. Because I had the best back bowl, I could drive on either hand, taking the jack through the head to the ditch. The problem was, this particular rink had me properly worried. The bias was terribly unpredictable. Sometimes, the bowl would hold away from the bias, while on other occasions it would bend like fury. If I pinned everything on line, and missed the jack, I was finished

'I chose option (c), and played with a yard on. The gods smiled on me – in a way I had not foreseen. I struck the shot bowl, cannoned on to the jack and sliced it towards my third bowl. I was home and dry, however precariously!'

'My opponent knew full well that I was very likely to sort out my problems on the forehand with my last bowl. I had the length, and he suspected that I would finally get it right. Therefore he had to draw close, and did so, on the backhand, skirting around his shot bowl and coming to within three inches of the jack'

'I had run out of tomorrows but not out of options. There were four: (a) A perfect forehand draw. Possible of course, but a tall order considering the difficulties I was having in finding the right line. (b) A rest shot to the shot bowl on the forehand. A better possibility than (a), but risky because I might come in a little wide and just trail the jack to my opponent's shot bowl. (c) A backhand shot with a little weight on the shot bowl. In its favour was the hand, which I felt

Chapter 4 SINGLES AND TEAM PLAY

A great deal of the tactical side of bowls is applicable to any playing configuration. Nevertheless, singles is quite a different game from pairs, and triples and fours are similarly distinctive in many respects. By analysing the peculiarities of each form of the game, you will be able to apply the general principles to the particular circumstances. Singles can be viewed as a gladiatorial contest without the bloodshed, while pairs is the most thorough test of your ability to forge a rewarding partnership. Triples and fours, especially the latter, put a high premium on your ability to function as a member of a team. And the various positions in a four, from lead through to skip, present you with quite different problems, challenges and rewards.

Singles play

Head-to-head confrontations have a particular fascination in any sport, and, as is the case with tennis, bowls singles is widely considered to be the most exciting form of the game. Certainly this is true from the spectator point of view, but most top-class bowlers too relish single-handed 'combat'. In a way it is simpler than the team game because there are none of the interactions and special demands of ensemble playing. As a singles player you are both lead and skip (the other team positions are not really reflected in singles play), so all your energies are focused on your own input. Being on your own in this situation may or may not bring out the best in you, but at least you always know where you are, and that you will stand or fall by your own efforts alone.

The draw shot is the most important in bowls generally, and it dominates the singles game even more than elsewhere. Day in, day out, the player who demonstrates more consistent skill with the draw will triumph over his opponents. The reason for this is that with only eight bowls in play, there is less scope for building the sort of complicated head

The finals of the 1984 Gateway Masters at Worthing – David Bryant, the eventual winner, watches New Zealander Peter Belliss

With England team manager Mike Jordan looking on, Senga McCrone of Scotland battles it out with Hong Kong's Joan Humphreys. Senga emerged as Commonwealth Games Singles Silver Medallist at Edinburgh in 1986

Mary Price of Buckinghamshire, one of England's leading outdoor singles players

The Queen congratulates England's Wendy Line on winning the singles gold medal in the 1986 Commonwealth Games

Singles play

that can be converted late in the end to yield a big score. Singles revolves around the steady accumulation of ones and twos, and the only way to be on the right side of those scores with any consistency is to get in first to the jack. Really good singles players tend to be useful skips, but they are invariably good leads (even if they rarely, if ever, play that position during their peak years). Conversely, a good lead is virtually bound to play a decent game of singles, because it is the essence of his game to build a solid foundation with his first two bowls. It is an old adage that a good lead will have the measure of a good skip at singles, and, while I do everything I can to refute it in every singles tournament I contest, I can appreciate the sentiment.

If I had ever entertained any doubts about the first two bowls being decisive in singles play (over the long haul of a tournament), they were conclusively resolved during the 1986 World Indoor Championships at Coatbridge, Scotland. I drew extremely well throughout, which meant that I was usually in the driving seat when it came to the latter half of the ends. I duly won the championship, and I did not have to look further than those opening two bowls to understand why.

Everything I have already said about tactics generally applies to singles. It is imperative to read the green quickly and determine your best hand. Get the line and get that first bowl close to the jack. Get the second bowl even closer, and then you can turn your attention to the way the head is shaping up. If your oppo-

nent outdraws you on the first bowl, get a second shot into the head before trying to convert. You will find the positional considerations later on in the end more congenial if you are already lying shot. Remember that the jack high bowl is an almost certain loser. Go easy on the heavier shots during the early stages.

Because your opponent is singular, you have ample opportunity to weigh him up. Look for his weaknesses and exploit them mercilessly. Make cunning use of mat and jack. You want a winning length for yourself and a losing length for him. Should these aims conflict, you will have to judge the maximum advantage for yourself. You will want to stick to a winning length, naturally, and change a losing

Is the jack long enough? In singles play you have only one opponent to consider as you attempt to pose an awkward length

length. If you are forging ahead, that is the length to stick with even if it is congenial for your opponent. It must be suiting you even better! If you are falling behind, change it, even if you cannot find a length that suits you better. What you must find, at all costs, is a length that disconcerts your opponent. You might not like the new length either, but there is a chance that you will settle in quicker.

Try to keep the pressure on your opponent from start to finish. This is particularly important in singles play because your target is a set score, not

Brian Duncan watches Jim Baker
play his opening bowl. The singles
game puts the greatest possible
premium on accurate draw play

superiority over a number of ends. In team play it is quite possible to build such an overwhelming lead that the latter stages of play become little more than a formality. Not so in singles, as every singles competitor will know to his cost. I have come back from a 19–6 deficit to win 21–20, and I have been overhauled after leading by 18–6. I once saw a good player lose 21–20 after leading 20–1.

Such dramatic comebacks as these are more likely to occur outdoors, where a sudden change in the elements can completely undo a player. As a rule, however, you will only let a really solid lead slip away from you by losing concentration – however slightly. If you let up on an opponent because you think you have done enough to win, you are suddenly vulnerable. If he gets even a glimmer of hope, just a hint of your waning resolve, it may be all he needs to galvanize himself for a decisive charge. The best tennis players are well known for their mental toughness when in sight of victory. If anything they increase the pressure on their hapless opponent. They want to hustle him off the court before he has time to mount a counterattack. Boxing provides an even starker example. The greatest boxers are said to possess a killer instinct. When they sense that they have their man going, they move in like a flash to finish him off – coolly, clinically, almost like an executioner. Such brutally expressed sentiments are a far cry from the language of the bowling green, but if you take competitive bowls seriously you will readily understand the relevance of the killer instinct.

Team play

Far and away the most common form of bowls is one or other of the team games – pairs, triples, and especially fours. This is partly because of the pressure on available greens, but also because the team games are so naturally suited to the convivial atmosphere of a club. A great many bowlers view the sport as a social recreation, one with a competitive edge, certainly, but not primarily as a means to realize sporting ambitions. Team bowls is perfectly geared to that approach, which is not to say that it is inferior to singles at the most fiercely competitive end of the spectrum. Competitive team bowling can be laced with high drama. It makes great technical and

England's 1984 World Championship squad, from the left: John Bell, Tony Allcock, Julian Haines, George Turley and David Bryant

emotional demands on the individual members, and a successful team can enjoy those pleasures of shared triumph that are unavailable to the singles player.

I will turn later to pairs and triples, because fours is the principal team game. Once you gain an understanding of the individual functions and tactical guidelines connected with fours, it is easy to apply this knowledge to the other team games.

A tense moment for Scotland and Ireland during the 1985 Home Internationals in Cardiff. Shot or not? Team play provides the opportunity to share the joys of success – and the pains of failure

Sally Smith of Norfolk in action during the county finals at Leamington Spa in 1985

Lead

From what I have said about the critical nature of the draw shot, it should come as no surprise when I say that the importance of the lead is impossible to overestimate. It is easy enough to underestimate, however, and it has been traditional to do so. The lead has been dismissed by bowlers who should know better as an unimaginative sort of chap who contents himself with bowling the jack to a length dictated by his skip, and then follows that with a couple of draw shots – early skirmishing, really, before the battle is fully joined. This is an utter travesty.

The lead must possess the qualities of concentration and persistence in full measure. He also needs mastery of the draw shot, which means, in effect, that he must be a very good bowler. The placing of the jack and those first two bowls, far from being a warming-up exercise, lay the foundation for the head. Any number 2 will tell you that there is all the difference in the world between coming to the mat with the head shaping nicely, and with it in sad disarray. By the time the leads have done their job, for good or ill, one side or the other will have an uphill task.

Because you have to learn to draw in order to learn to bowl, the position of lead is the natural one for the novice to concentrate on. There is a tendency, however, for learners to aspire to positions down the order as their skills begin to develop. This ambition is generally abetted at club level, where the chance to play at number 2 or 3 is viewed as a promotion – a reward for success in the lead position. This might seem natural

enough, and it is undeniable that at club level a lead's lot can be unenviable, especially if he is showing real promise. It can be soul-destroying to keep sending down accurate opening bowls, only to find your painstakingly acquired positional advantage squandered by mediocre, or even inept team members further down the order.

The answer to this dilemma is not, in my opinion, for the talented lead to seek immediate promotion in the order, tempting though that may be. What he should do is to demonstrate such ability in the lead position that he becomes snapped up by a better team. Playing at lead in a class rink is anything but boring. The draw shot is the most satisfying in the game, and it is the special preserve of the lead. If your long-term goal is to become a skip, at any level, you need as thorough a grounding as you can get in the fundamentals of the game. The draw shot is the bedrock of bowls, and you can never learn enough about it, let alone too much. A good lead will always be in demand, and it is commonly said that the surest route to an international career is through the lead position.

Consider my own experience. I attempted to gain a place in the England team on four consecutive occasions between 1974 and 1977, variously at the number 2 and 3 positions. I failed each time, and then in 1978 I made a decision that was, in retrospect, pivotal to my career. I decided that my best chance of gaining a full cap was as a lead. I tried for that position and got it, and I have never looked back.

Some of the finest leads go further than I did. Because lead is the only specialist position in a team (relying, as it does, on the draw shot exclusively), it can be a real challenge to stick with it. For a perfectionist, it can be a lifetime pursuit. Brett Morley of Nottinghamshire is a very talented young lead who shows no inclination to move down the order, which he could easily do. John Ottaway of Norfolk is currently England's most successful lead, indoors and out, and it would be difficult to imagine him ever having to struggle to keep that position in a team at any level.

A good lead will bring the same conscientious attitude to the early stages of a match that the good singles player does. He will learn what he can from the trial ends, settle into line and length as soon as he conceivably can, select the better hand and watch his opposite number like a hawk. Indeed he will take the keenest interest in all proceedings, looking for telltale clues to the running of the green, peculiarities of mat and jack positions, anything at all that can aid him in laying that foundation for a favourable head. 'Foundation' is the important concept here, as it is with opening batsmen in cricket. The lead will worry less about lying shot at the end of his stint than he will about having two useful bowls in the head. There should be ample opportunity for his successors to convert the head at an appropriate moment. The lead's aim is to make that task as easy as possible – or, at least, no more difficult than necessary! He will be at pains not to take too narrow a line to the jack (usually a wasted bowl) or to bowl short when the shot lies against him. He will of course avoid bowling jack high, and he will strive to keep the target area narrow when he is lying shot. In other words, he will not broaden the head with his second shot if he has succeeded in drawing with the first. If, on the other hand, his opponent has a winning first draw he should play right to it or alongside it, so as to broaden the target for his number 2. He will certainly resist any temptation to have a go at removing an opposition bowl. That is not his task, and should he attempt it and fail he will only be able to watch forlornly as his team-mates struggle to repair the damage.

It goes without saying that the lead must be expert at casting the jack to a length (usually one dictated by his skip). I used to practise endlessly with the jack in my early days, and I rarely see that done by aspiring leads. Take my advice and practise with the jack until casting it to a length becomes absolutely ingrained in you.

Brett Morley (top right) of Nottingham is one of the game's finest specialist leads. It was as lead that Tony Allcock first gained international status. Grant Knox (right), leading for Scotland against Hong Kong at Balgreen in 1986, resorts to the tape measure

Number 2

Before turning to the playing function of the number 2, it is worth noting that he must shoulder an official duty. Under IBB rules, he 'shall keep a record of all shots scored for and against his side and shall at all times retain possession of the score card while play is in progress. He shall see that the names of all players are entered on the score card, shall compare his record of the game with that of the opposing second player as each end is declared, and at the close of the game shall hand his score card to his skip.'

Having disposed of that, what are the really important duties of the number 2, so often the forgotten man in fours? They are, in fact, extremely onerous, and it is completely mistaken to treat this position as a harmless haven for the beginner, an error frequently committed by club selectors. The reason this happens, presumably, is because lead is a specialist position, while the best and most experienced bowlers tend to gravitate to the number 3 and skip positions. Such a process of selection leaves the number 2 as rather an afterthought. I disagree entirely with such a policy, and would always put my least experienced bowler team member in at lead. This is partly for his sake – since he must gain proficiency with the draw shot, whatever his goal – and partly for the team's sake. The number 2 position is far too demanding for the novice.

Consider his role. To begin with, he is invariably having to deal with a situation not of his own making. If his lead has done well, the number 2 will be attempting to consolidate the posi-tion, which means bowling to blank positions. He may be instructed by his skip to protect the existing shot (or shots), to add to them or simply to provide long-term insurance for a potential winning head. The number 2 must therefore be a good draw player, and in particular he must have accurate length. If his lead has laid a solid foundation, it is up to him to begin laying the bricks. Given that the head he is bowling to may be any which way, he must be adaptable enough to play either hand in either direction, which means he must be an extremely quick as well as accurate student of the green.

The situation is entirely different if his lead has left things in a bit of a mess. If his lead has not got close to the jack, it is up to the number 2 to put things to rights by drawing right into the head. He is the last member of his side to be guaranteed a clear shot at the jack, so he is under considerable pressure. If he fails, following his lead's failure, the end may be beyond redemption. Drawing well under pressure is therefore a prerequisite in this position, but that is by no means all. The number 2 may be required to play any of the running shots, on any hand. In fact he may be required to do practically anything under the bowling sun, and the shrewdest observers of the game have always been at pains to point out that the number 2 is really

Julian Haines (centre) played at number 2, with John Bell (far left) and George Turley in the England triples team for the 1986 Commonwealth Games

Annette Evans played at number 2 in Scotland's gold medal quartet in the 1985 World Championships

the anchorman of the side. W. J. Emmett, an English international of the 1920s, put it clearly enough when he said: 'I am afraid too little importance is attached to the number 2 player. The position is often thought of as a stop-gap and the passenger of the rink, whilst in reality it should be filled with a player of wide experience in order to force or direct the game.' My sentiments exactly.

There is a very useful practice routine specifically geared to improving the tactical understanding of anyone playing in the second position, and it is most useful from the singles standpoint as well. Set up a mock head with four bowls (including two of your own) without giving much thought to the actual positioning. Then go back to the mat and examine all the options available to you. Work out the percentage shot and play it. Draw any relevant conclusions, and then repeat the exercise into a different head.

As an example of the contribution a good number 2 can make, I cite Julian Haines of Berkshire, who played with me in the 1984 World Championships in Aberdeen. This example may also give you some indication of the extreme demands that a beleaguered skip will make when it comes to the crunch! As we battled it out with Canada on our way to the gold medal, on three consecutive occasions I asked Julian to drive at the jack. On each occasion he drove the jack into the ditch, with his bowl resting inches from it. We duly won, but I shudder to think what would have happened if my number 2 had been the weak link in the chain.

Number 3

In that picturesque winter game of curling, analogous to bowling in so many ways, the third player is called vice-skip. That strikes me as a completely accurate description of the function of the number 3, and I would not object in the slightest if bowls were to borrow that nomenclature from its icy cousin. The number 3 is the skip's right hand – and his eyes and ears and any other sense organs that might be attuned to a match. He is, or at least should be, 'the great communicator'.

The number 3 position, in terms of what the player uniquely contributes to the team effort, is the hardest to describe. That is not because it is in any sense vague, but because the essential character of the role is inevitably coloured by the personality of the skip. The ideal number 3 must of course be a good all-round bowler, but he must be much more than that. He must complement the skip as only a genuine partner can do. He must at all times demonstrate absolute faith in his skip's judgment, while at the same time resisting the easy option of becoming a 'yes' man. He must, in other words, respect his skip without being overawed by him.

Such a relationship must be honestly based, never contrived for convenience or the sake of an easy life. If a number 3 lacks confidence in his skip, he should aim to join a rink whose skip he does respect. Otherwise he will become disillusioned, defeatist, and a millstone round his team's neck.

Mike Jordan regularly partners Tony Allcock at number 3. The number 3 must provide the skip with sound advice, while at the same time remembering that the skip must retain overall responsibility

This may sound a tall order, and so it is. It means that a number 3 who is perfectly suited to one skip will not be to another, and vice versa. And because the personality of good skips varies so widely, it is impossible to be precise about the personal qualities that make a good number 3. As a generalization, however, it is safe to say that he should be a lively, outgoing type as opposed to a self-contained introvert. He should provide encouragement and support to those above himself in the order as well as to the skip. With the latter, he must be a shrewd judge of when to speak his mind, and when to remain silent, so as not to cause unnecessary distraction – especially at a critical juncture. In the best partnerships, the number 3 and the skip seem to have an uncanny knack of unspoken communication.

With Mike Jordan, who partners me regularly at number 3, I have achieved an enviable rapport. This did not come overnight, nor indeed could it have. We made our mistakes in our early days together, learned from them, and of course we learned from each other. He manages me beautifully! He seems to know exactly the moment to offer me badly needed advice, and, just as important, when to keep his doubts to himself and let me exercise my prerogative as skip without hindrance. He also acts as an essential filter between me and the other players on the team. Ideally, the skip should be closely involved with each of his players, but it is inevitable that he should communicate most closely with the number 3. The number 3, therefore, must be able to take messages up the line as well as *down*. A thoughtful skip will want to know the mood and the minds of those for whom he is responsible, even though he has plenty to be preoccupied with himself. The number 3 is his chief intelligence officer.

On a technical level, the number 3 should possess all the shots (like the skip). It is especially important that he be a good judge of weight, because he is forever called upon to play positional shots, yard ons, blocking shots, not to mention trailing the jack, and, not infrequently, full-blooded drives. If you are beginning to get the impression that a good number 3 should be a paragon, you are not far wrong.

A good number 3 at work – Sammy Allen of Ireland giving his assessment of the situation to his skip Jim Baker

Skip

There have been analogies drawn between the skip's role and many other demanding activities, but I think the most illuminating is its likeness to conducting an orchestra. All the individual members of the orchestra know how to play their instruments, and they are all familiar with the music they are playing. Left to their own devices, they would be pretty certain of getting through to the end without making a real hash of it. It is just an amusing fallacy that the orchestra would immediately fall into disarray, producing an anarchy of noise, if the conductor should lay down his baton and walk away.

What, then, is the function of the conductor? If the players can play the music in time without the discipline of the baton, what is his contribution? It is this. The conductor has particular insights into the music, and he knows the musical effect he is trying to achieve. He well knows the abilities (and limitations) of the various sections of the orchestra, and even of its individual musicians. He also knows the acoustical peculiarities of the concert hall. His

Everyone is in on the act, as Wales play Scotland. The rival skips, however, carry the burden of decision

task is to get the finest possible result using the means at his disposal. During rehearsals he will articulate his wishes, encourage, criticize, cajole, inspire – he will use whatever is in his musical and personal armoury to communicate his vision to the players. When it comes to the performance, he is restricted to using the baton, with as much body language as he chooses. This is, however, only a refined version of what he was doing in rehearsals. He has the conception, unique to himself, and he can only realize it through the combined efforts of others, and that is only possible if the others understand what he

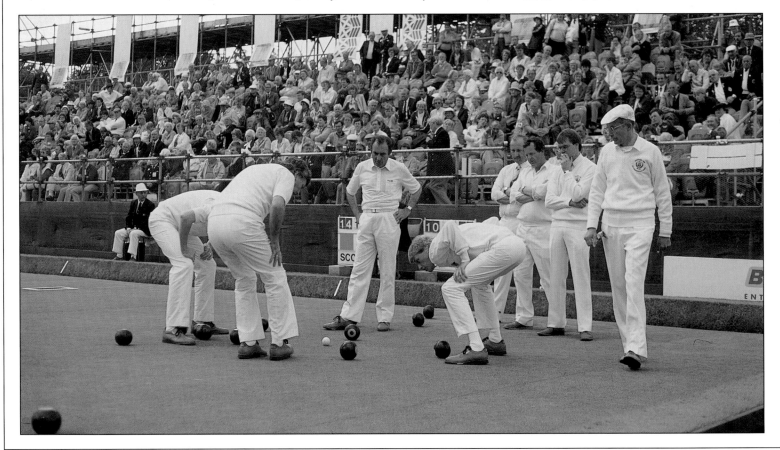

is striving for. For everyone's sake, there can only be one vision, one conductor.

It may seem rather high-flown to suggest parallels between such a maestro and a bowls skip, but I believe they are there. The skip is the leader of a team of individuals, individuals with special skills, known limitations and all the rest of it. At an advanced level, the players are expert at what they do, and they most certainly do not need their skip to teach them how to suck eggs. They can assess the running of the green as ably as he can, and their tactical knowledge may easily equal his. Percentage play, the balance between attack and defence, the need to rise to the challenge of the pressure shot – these things are the common coinage of top-class bowls.

The proper function of the skip is to provide purposeful direction. He must harness the talents, the energies and the ambitions of his team-mates so as to achieve victory, and to do that effectively he needs to combine strategic vision with tactical astuteness. In that, he is like the conductor. But he has to do more as well. Not only must he direct operations, he must pull his weight as a player – more than his weight, when the chips are down. He must provide leadership by example, he must inspire by deeds as well as words.

Everything that has been said about the need of the number 3 to be a good communicator applies to the skip. Some skips are naturally more outgoing than others, but whatever their temperamental make-up they must be receptive to advice, as well as articulate in giving it. While it is with his number 3 that the skip needs the most intimate communication during matchplay, I find it natural as well as sound policy to remain in close contact with the other members as well. This is partly a matter of morale – providing encouragement, praising good shots and sympathizing with difficulties, just keeping them in the picture and fully involved – but it is also a considerable help to me personally. The lead may well have spotted something in the green that I have

Tony Allcock instructs his lead during the 1985 Gateway Masters pairs. The skip's directions to his team-mates must be crystal clear

overlooked, the number 2 may have glimpsed a weakness in his opposite number that we can exploit, and so forth. This is not to recommend uninhibited chatter, but is meant rather as an acknowledgement that a skip needs all the help he can get, and he should not be hidebound about its source.

Skip

Beyond such general comments about a constructive working relationship between the skip and his colleagues, it is possible to be a little more specific if we look at each team member in turn, as he and the skip relate to each other.

While the lead casts the jack, it is accepted that the skip should, if he chooses, dictate the length. The length of jack is an overall tactical consideration, of relevance to the whole team, so it is reasonable that the skip should be involved. In choosing the length, he will have a number of things in mind. As the match wears on, he will have developed a good idea of how the length of jack is relating to either side's performance, and like a singles player he will determine jack length accordingly. Unlike the singles player, however, he will not be swayed solely by how he himself and his opposing skip are performing, but also by how jack length is affecting the teams as a whole. This is a critical distinction. If, for example, I am on sparkling form and have justification for thinking that my bowls as skip are likely to be decisive, come what may, then I will be inclined to choose a jack length that suits me ideally. However, if, under the circumstances, I think my playing contribution is of less importance to the outcome, I might well bow to the fact that, on *his* preferred length, my lead is drawing with deadly accuracy and thereby providing an excellent foundation for the head. This may be a difficult judgment to make objectively, but that is precisely the sort of situation in which a good skip shows his mettle. A team game has no place

In this Middleton Cup match (1983), the skip has instructed his lead to move the mat right forward

for prima donnas in any position, and there is nothing worse than a skip who cannot resist playing to the gallery – consciously or unconsciously willing on the awkward head which he, and he alone, can salvage with a brilliant last bowl. A skip who likes to show off in this way will quickly and deservedly lose the respect of his team.

There are occasions for letting the lead choose his own length of jack, and some skips are more relaxed about this than others. At the beginning of a match, for example, I might

have no fixed plan, and no firm ideas about the running of the green. While I would not want my lead to cast a short jack to begin with (it is always a good idea to determine the maximum draw early on), I might not have any real conviction about the exact length. I would therefore be inclined to let the lead decide for himself. Similarly, if we are playing to a winning length, my lead will need no instruction not to change it. Generally, however, leads prefer the skip to stand for the jack rather than to cast to a blank position. As for deciding on mat placement, exactly the same considerations apply as apply to the jack.

Having cast the jack, the lead's role is clear enough. He plays the two best draw shots he can muster – on the hand of his choice. If my lead is having difficulty finding the line, and I think I have a helpful suggestion to make, then I will do so. Simply to point out the obvious – that he is drawing poorly – would be pointless, and probably counterproductive. The skip should always try to encourage his colleagues, and, while this does not rule out constructive criticism, it certainly does rule out ungracious whining about missed chances.

The collaboration between the skip and the number 2 is rather different. It is at this point that the skip will begin to direct the shape of the head, and therefore he will have definite ideas about what the number 2 should attempt. He will, after inspecting the head and perhaps consulting the number 3, direct the number 2's shot. Naturally he will bear in mind the individual's strengths and weaknesses, as well as the state of the head, but, having weighed the situation as best he can, he must decide on the course of action. Admittedly, there are circumstances in which the number 2 has an obvious shot to play, and instruction between players familiar with each other is unnecessary, but the point remains that the skip should, at this stage, be fully involved with his tactical responsibility. And he should be on the look-

out, too, for any practical help he can give the number 2. If, for example, he is consistently bowling short, the skip might think it prudent to stand a couple of feet behind the position he actually wants the bowl to arrive at, hoping thereby to encourage a delivery that drops on a length. That is likely to be more effective than spelling out the obvious error, which could all too easily result in over-bowling.

With his number 3, the skip is dealing with his closest associate, like the conductor with the leader of the

The Canadian skip Dan Milligan explains his reading of the situation to his lead John Simmons, during the 1986 Gateway Masters pairs

Skip

orchestra. The skip and number 3 spend a lot of time together examining the head, and chatting quietly at the side of the rink about the state of play. Because of this close, continuous contact, it is more a matter of the two of them coming to an agreement about what the number 3 should do when it is his turn to play, rather than a unilateral decision by the skip. Clearly his must, where necessary, be the decisive voice, since his is the responsibility, but a sensible skip would not lightly insist on his number 3 playing a shot against his better judgment. Should it come to that, however, the number 3 must swallow his reservations, and go to the mat fully committed to his skip's decision. That is the only way that the relationship between the two can function properly. There cannot be two skips.

When it comes to the skip's bowls, the relationship between him and the number 3 shifts subtly. It is highly appropriate for the number 3 to offer advice, although of course he can hardly insist that it be taken. Because the skip's bowls are so critical, it is an inflexible rule that he should not go to the mat before he is completely certain in his own mind that he is playing the right shot. He cannot, like those before him, acquiesce to someone else's judgment. Whatever the process of deliberation, and with whomever, he has no skip to share his responsibility if it turns out to be a

Jubilation for the English trio of Wynne Richards, Martin Sekjer and David Bryant, as skip David Ward plays a winning shot

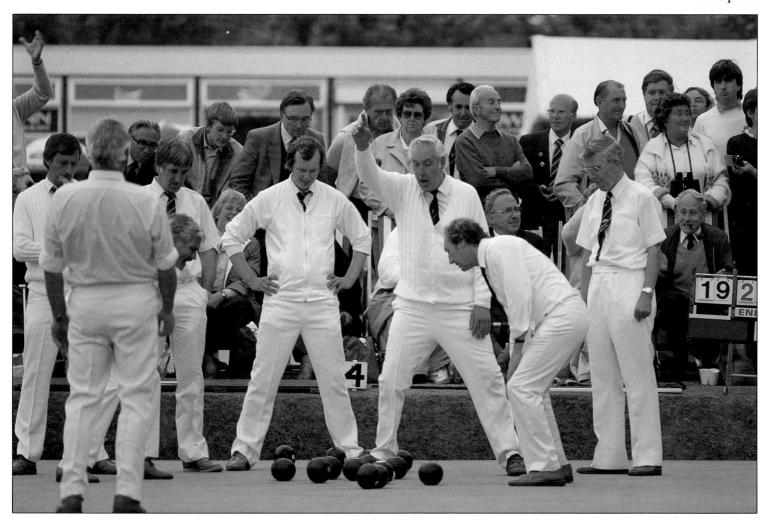

hideous mistake. This can put the number 3 in a tricky position. On the one hand, he will quite properly want to give his skip the best advice he can, knowing that his skip expects that advice. On the other, he must be able to determine the point at which his skip's mind is settled on a particular course of action. Then, it would be quite inappropriate for the number 3 to continue to press counter-arguments, since that would only serve to cloud the issue, and perhaps cause prolonged indecision and even irritation. Fine distinctions between the merits of rival choices of shot are of less importance than the frame of mind in which the skip goes to the mat. He must be resolved and confident, and it is the number 3's task to ensure that he is so.

The more able the skip, the more soundly will he harmonize his roles as leader and player. While never forgetting the decisive contribution he can make with his bowls, he will be continuously mindful that, in a team game, team effort alone can bring sustained success. And team effort, while it is certainly bound up with tactics, can only be fully exploited if it is a natural, spontaneous expression of team morale. A skip who neglects morale, for any reason, is at least temporarily skipping badly. We have all done it.

Skip

On one occasion I was skipping a four from my own club, Cheltenham, in a county competition. My lead, Keith Ward, was badly off form, playing his bowls all over the place and thereby putting the number 2, and eventually the rest of us, under undue pressure. Even so, we were much the better side and should have been able to cope with the situation. We did not, losing by the odd shot.

By the end I was in a pretty foul mood, and in the dressing-room afterwards I was grumbling about our miserable performance. Any way you cared to look at it, we had let ourselves down badly, losing a close match to opponents who could only have envisaged victory in their dreams. What did we think we were playing at out there? I was interrupted in my bleak analysis by Keith, who knew perfectly well that my strictures, though addressed to us all, myself included, really were mainly directed at him. It was he, after all, who had started the rot by bowling so poorly.

To my astonishment, Keith suddenly rounded on me. Where I might have expected contrition, I suddenly found myself on the receiving end of a different, quite unwelcome interpretation of the match. 'Actually,' he said, 'if you could have seen your face while we were playing, then you would realize why we lost the game.' This blunt criticism perplexed me at the time, and it hurt me too. How unjust, I thought, and I set off for home in a mood of deepening gloom. The weather matched my mood, cold and wet, as it had been during the match just to compound our miseries.

As I was driving through the rain, however, I kept returning to Keith's comment. It slowly dawned on me that maybe he had a point, and once I allowed that possibility my entire defence crumbled away. The evening's proceedings took on a different perspective. And the truth, when I saw it, was unflattering. This is what had actually happened. I had come to the match after a difficult day at work which had left me rather jaded. The rotten weather had compounded my unhappiness. And when, to cap it all, my lead began to bowl like a novice, I had succumbed to the weight of negative factors bearing down on me. I had allowed a bad day to deteriorate into a wretched evening, with scarcely a protest.

What I should have done was relegate my worries firmly to the back of my mind as I walked on to the green. As for the rain trickling down the back of my neck, so what? How often have I played and won in such conditions, and, if I really cannot abide inclement weather, why am I playing bowls rather than skittles? Free from such foolish distractions, I would then have focused my attention on the one relevant consideration – namely, that my lead was getting off to a terrible start. That is always cause for alarm, and it calls for remedial action. It calls, to be precise, for the skip's immediate attention. I should

At any level of competition, bowls should be exhilarating and sheer fun. One of the skip's most important duties is to ensure the high morale of the team

have been looking for the reasons, offering advice and encouragement, scurrying up and down the rink clapping my team-mates on. There was probably nothing wrong with Keith that evening that a bit of decent skipping would not have sorted out quickly enough (which of course was what he was hoping for). Certainly, however weakly he was going to play that night, I should have been able to contain the damage. I should have exerted myself fully to ensure that the rot did not spread to the numbers 2 and 3, and I should have composed myself for the unexpected burden of having to bowl to the best of my ability against mediocre opposition. All in all, I should have behaved like a skip instead of sulking like Achilles, without even the comfort of a tent. It was a salutary lesson, and I determined then and there never again to court defeat by allowing myself to tackle the skip's duties in a sullen manner.

Being carpeted by your lead is not a skip's ideal form of off-green team talk, but it served its purpose. During play, it is quite impracticable for a skip to attempt to conduct operations in a democratic manner, because that would imply a natural right of dissent, and dissent would result in chaos. The situation is entirely different in the clubhouse, or it should be. Frank talk between colleagues is to be positively encouraged, and only a pig-headed skip would view probing questions about the whys and wherefores of his decision-making as mutinous. I am no believer in the sort of post mortems that degenerate into pointless breast-beating and futile recrimination, but cogent discussion of team tactics is likely to be illuminating – as indeed it was on this inauspicious occasion!

A final point about communication between skip and team concerns precise instructions. In 1986 I attended a seminar given by Jimmy Davidson, the England national coach. There were many internationals in attendance, and, in the course of a single morning of discussion, shot analysis and tactical debate, it became increasingly clear to me that even the most experienced skips can be woefully imprecise in their use of language. This is particularly noticeable over the yard on shot. Because it is a handy phrase, and an accepted description of a particular type of shot, we tend to use it to embrace significantly different intentions. It is all too common for us to ask for a yard on when we actually mean two yards, or even three. Our team-mates have enough to contend with as it is, and it seems unreasonable to expect them to add mind-reading to their bowling skills.

Pairs and triples

I enjoy pairs immensely. It provides close comradeship on the green, without anything like the burden of man-management imposed by fours. The establishing of a successful partnership, however, can be a delicate business. Ideally, the two players should be complementary. One should be an exemplary lead, the other a natural skip. The number 2 and 3 roles really do not apply here, or in the sense that they do they are subsumed respectively by the lead and the skip. The skip must be in overall command as much as he is in fours, so it is essential that the lead not feel an urge to vie with him. Whatever position he may play in fours, the lead in pairs must be happy with this arrangement. It follows from this that there is a tendency in pairs to match players of varying experience – the more with the less, the senior with the junior. Compatibility can outweigh sheer bowling ability in pairs, and rivalry must be avoided under any circumstances.

Having said that, it might appear an ironic contradiction that David Bryant and I frequently partner each other. We are both experienced skips, and therefore both of us consider it normal and natural to be in charge of a rink. How do we manage it? Specifically, how do we decide which of us is to skip the rink? The answer is that we manage very well, and our allocation of roles is viewed by us both as a tactical consideration, not a personal one. We entered the 1986 World Indoor Pairs Championship with David as skip. Our reasoning was that because I was in such good form with the draw shot we should exploit that by putting me in as lead. Since either

George Adrain of Scotland issues clear instructions to team-mate Grant Knox, on their way to the pairs gold medal in the 1986 Commonwealth Games

Tony Allcock and David Bryant (opposite) with their trophy for retaining the World Indoor Pairs title in 1987. While both are vastly experienced skips, David at lead with Tony skipping is the winning combination

Tony Allcock and his partner Pat Bradley pose with fellow competitors in the 1986 McCarthy and Stone mixed pairs

Pairs and triples

of us was perfectly happy to play under the other as skip, that single reason was perfectly adequate. In the event, we lost our opening match against Bill Boettger and Ronnie Jones of Canada, but mercifully the competition was then made up of a round robin at the preliminary stage. We were still alive after that defeat, and because we were disappointed with our play we decided to swap positions. We went on to win the title, and this year we will enter with me as skip again – simply because we do not intend to tamper with a winning combination.

It is not all that common for a partnership to swap around in this way, mainly because most pairs tournaments are knockouts from the start, so there is no chance for such improvisation. Even the World Indoor Pairs Championship has now adopted the knockout formula, so if we start badly this year we will not have this option. Also, if a partnership is really based

Studies in concentration. Tony Allcock and his partner David Bryant take a rather serious look at the competition during the 1986 World Indoor Pairs Championship. The marker John Kirkwood shares their interest

on a blend of leading and skipping skills, such a change would not suggest itself. David and I are simply fortunate in feeling at home in either position.

The essential clue to such a partnership as ours, however, is that we are scrupulous about keeping to our positions, whichever they might be. As singles competitors and rival skips, we view each other as peers. However, when we have settled on our playing order in pairs, the skip is the skip. Obviously, when I am skipping I am extremely keen on David's advice at every stage, and he is not reticent about giving it. But he is invariably at pains to point out that his advice is simply that, and that as skip I must play my own game. I cannot duck my responsibility just because I am playing alongside David Bryant. With our roles reversed, he in turn must shoulder that burden.

Triples is so similar to fours from the tactical standpoint as not to require separate consideration. The lead and skip have no need to adapt their games at all, although the second man will find that some aspects of the game are reminiscent of the number 2 position in fours, and others of the number 3 position. The aspect of triples that attracts most general discussion, perhaps, is the number of bowls. Because each player bowls three, there can be up to eighteen bowls in the head. There is occasional grumbling that this leads to a game of smash and grab rather than skill, and many players would welcome the elimination of the third bowl, thereby bringing the total in play down to twelve.

There are those who think the triples game would be improved by reducing the number of bowls per player from three to two. As it is, the head can get rather crowded with a possible eighteen bowls in contention

Women's and mixed bowls

In most competitive sports, physical strength is a sufficiently significant factor to have a bearing on an individual's performance. The fit male tends to be both larger and more muscular than his female counterpart, and the advantage in strength this provides not only assures him a competitive edge (if both possess equivalent skill), it necessarily has tactical implications. In golf, for example, no woman, however gifted, would even dream of attempting to reach the green with an iron from a fairway position 250 yards away. A glance at Greg Norman's shoulders would tell her why a shot that was a realistic possibility for him was out of the question for her. Her tactics would of necessity reflect her physical capabilities.

Bowls is one of those sports in which the element of skill so far outweighs brute strength that the latter becomes almost irrelevant. Whatever part strength plays in the game (and fierce driving in the heaviest conditions requires considerable strength), it is not of sufficient importance to affect tactics. Therefore, the women's game can be taken as a mirror image of the men's, and the tactics of winning bowls as universally applicable.

Because my mother was an England international, I have had long observation of women's bowls, and I consider the qualities that distinguish it from the men's game to be interesting. On the positive side, skilful women bowlers tend to excel at the draw shot, and because I put such a high premium on drawing I admire that characteristic. I do, however, have one general criticism to make of women's bowls, and I hope it will be taken in the fraternal manner in which it is intended.

I believe that women tend to be a little too reliant on the draw shot. This tendency dampens down the adventurous side of the game, instilling an attitude of undue caution. From caution, it is a short step to negative play – where the desire to avoid mistakes outweighs the desire to achieve results. I am well aware that any such generalization is open to challenge. I can think of many excellent women skips who display an attractive, attacking style, and do so to great effect. When the situation calls for it, they drive just as aggressively as the rest of us. But I stand by my general comment. Far too often, I hear skips urging caution – phrasing their instructions negatively, as in: 'We have the best three back bowls, but if you slice the jack to the right we

Western Samoa's delightful Pativaine Ainuu during the 1982 Commonwealth Games at Brisbane

Freda Elliott (bottom) has a sisterly word with Irish team-mate Margaret Johnston on their way to the 1986 Commonwealth Pairs gold medal

Norma Shaw (below), one of the world's top women players and a formidable opponent for any man

Welsh skip Linda Parker applauds this effort by Rita Jones against Ireland. Good team spirit is an essential ingredient of successful and enjoyable bowls

Women's and mixed bowls

might lose two shots.' This might be perfectly true, but how different the complexion would be if the attitude adopted were more positive: 'We have the best three back bowls – go for the jack, and if your own bowl comes with it we shall be four.' Even to mention the possibility of slicing the jack is to put a negative construction on what should be seen as a positive opportunity. Obviously, *anything* can happen in bowls. Disaster always lurks, but fear of disaster does not ward it off; it is dispiriting and debilitating.

If I were coaching women, that is, women who wanted to make their mark at a competitive level, this is the area I would concentrate on most. I would assume that they would find neither more nor less difficulty than men in mastering the technical side of the game. As for appreciating tactical considerations, that is simply a matter of intelligence applied to experience. But I would positively encourage aggression, in the tactical context. I would not suggest that the keen woman bowler model herself on Rob Parrella, but I would suggest that she accept the challenge and reap the rewards of an attacking game. If Martina Navratilova were to take up bowls, I suspect that she would do rather well.

On further reflection, perhaps we men should refrain from giving the women any encouragement whatsoever. Early in 1987 I was unceremoniously bundled out of the opening round of an invitation tournament (the Samson Bowls Classic) by Norma Shaw. Norma, a former World Outdoor Champion, has

become a serious threat to any of us indoors, especially at the Darlington club which she knows so well. She now has my scalp to add to Willie Wood's and Jim Baker's, and the three of us are thinking of ordering tee shirts emblazoned with 'Norma rules OK!' In time, I fear that quite a few more of the leading men players will

Norma Shaw bowls against David Bryant in the 1984 Superbowl

be entitled to wear one.

I feel obliged to add a sobering postscript to my defeat at Norma's hands. She thoroughly deserved her victory, but one aspect of the experience gave me cause for concern. The

Merle Richardson looks on as her rival Willie Wood bowls. One of the attractions of the sport is that women and men can compete on level terms

Darlington spectators were proudly partisan, and they had come to cheer their heroine on to victory. This was entirely understandable and I was prepared for it. Norma is almost a local, she was inevitably a bit of an underdog against the reigning World Champion, and she was of course competing on equal terms with a man. So far so good. What I was not prepared for, however, was the occasional barracking I received as I stood on the mat preparing to bowl. There were people in the crowd clearly exercising their vocal ingenuity as best they could to put me off my shot.

I am not easily goaded, and I am lucky to possess fairly steady nerves. Nevertheless, I would not be telling the truth if I were to dismiss such shenanigans as an irrelevance. They did not help my concentration, to put it mildly, and I was reminded of Greg Norman's recent altercations with similarly unsporting spectators on American golf courses. I then returned to my hotel room and switched on the televised snooker. As if to reinforce my displeasure, and my fears for the future of the game I love, there were Jimmy White and Tony Meo having to cope with the same sort of boorish crowd behaviour. Games of touch and skill require concentration. They are not like all-in wrestling, and, if rowdy partisanship on the part of even a tiny minority of spectators should become the trend of the future, it can only have a deleterious effect on the standards of performance — and on the enjoyment of the vast majority of true supporters who revel in fair combat, keenly contested in a sporting manner.

Chapter 5 THE INNER GAME

Competition bowls, like any sport, makes mental and emotional as well as physical demands. The successful player will not, under any circumstances, fall victim to muddled thinking or indecision. He will have his wits about him at all times, weighing the options coolly and executing the chosen shot with resolution and single-minded determination. The ability to cope with pressure is an equally important part of the inner game. Some players thrive on pressure, and are able to produce their finest efforts at the most critical junctures. Others, equally skilled, seem to cave in when the pressure becomes intense. It is arguable the extent to which mental toughness is innate and the degree to which it can be acquired, but anyone serious about competing at bowls must examine that quality in relation to the game as a whole.

The role of practice

I must preface these comments on practice by confessing to a curious ambiguity on the subject. On the one hand, I believe that you simply must go out of your way to make time for constructive practice if you want to achieve much in the game. On the other, I keep it to a minimum myself, and have done so during the period in which I have enjoyed my greatest success. I believe that I can explain this paradox, although it may appear to be more like a sleight of hand attempt to explain it away. If that is so, and it comes down to a choice between doing what I say and what I do, stick with the former every time.

You can take it as read that you will learn most of whatever you do learn about the game of bowls in the course of play. The preceding chapters were primarily intended to enable you to accelerate and extend that natural learning curve, but here I want to examine the merits of practice. They are twofold. First, practice is the quickest, surest method of gaining a sound technique. It is only under practice conditions that you can isolate the various aspects of the delivery, and repeat them time after time until you get them right. Any example would do, but it will be obvious

that if you have a chronic problem with hooking your forehand, the practice green is the proper place to sort it out. You need to straighten out your delivery, and you are far better off trying to do so when that is your sole concern, rather than muck about with it in the course of a game.

Second, practice gives you the best opportunity of deepening your tactical understanding of the game. You

Hardly the regulation dress for assorted celebrities as they warm up for a match. A little practice and a lot of optimism may not put them in the Allcock class, but they can dream

will frequently find yourself in puzzling situations – situations in which it is not at all clear what shot you should attempt, or having played a shot as you intended you have been surprised by the result, or having opted for one shot, you have been curious as to what would have happened had you chosen another. This puzzlement can have endless permutations, and no matter how experienced you become you will never be entirely free of it. But constructive practice can help. You can create typical heads, or recreate as best you can actual ones, analyse them, play your shot and note the result. Then you can put the bowls back into position and play it again, differently. If you get into the habit of doing this you will begin to build up a memory bank, and memory plays a very large part in bowls. It may be perfectly true to say that no two heads are ever quite the same, but when you have played as much as I have they tend to have a pretty familiar look to them. I may never have been exactly there before, but I have been somewhere thereabouts, and I know that I am constantly drawing on my memory bank, whether consciously or not. Memory may be imperfect, but it is a far better guide than guesswork. It should be your aim to banish guesswork as completely as possible. If during matchplay you can combine attentiveness with mentally stimulating practice, you will be able to turn your experience to maximum advantage. The heedless player writes his mishaps off to experience and forgets; the wise one puts them down to experience and remembers.

More and more clubs are encouraging youngsters, which is a most healthy development. This lad is engaged in the serious matter of getting his jack centred at St Neots in Cambridgeshire

Israel's Cecil Bransky (below), in stark contrast to Tony Allcock, thrives on practice. Getting the balance right between matchplay and practice is a decidedly individual matter

How I learned to bowl

Few of you will have been born into the game of bowls in the nearly literal sense that I was. Both my parents were county bowlers, and my mother went on to become an England international. During the summer of 1955, when I was born, my mother was engaged in competition both before and after that event. Indeed, shortly after, with me in oblivious attendance, she won her club pairs title. I can therefore claim that my first appearance in a tournament was in the 1955 Goodwood Ladies Bowling Club Championships.

Because my parents were such keen bowlers, and I was an only child, I have many childhood memories of the bowling club environment. Sometimes I contented myself with watching, but often, armed with a set of small woods, I could create the illusion of participating by bowling away on a piece of rough ground to the side of the green. My parents did not in any way encourage me to take an interest in the game, but the circumstances of such a childhood obviously steered me in that direction. And when, at the age of fourteen, I decided to apply myself seriously to the game, there is no doubt that this long, passive apprenticeship served me well. I had already absorbed a sound enough understanding of the tactics to enable me to apply my technical skills, as they developed, to maximum advantage. It gave me a head start over my peers, and I enjoyed considerable success as a junior.

During those teenage years I practised like a demon. I loved the game

both for its intrinsic beauty and for the outlet it provided for my competitive urge. I knew that I was lucky enough to possess natural ability, and I was strongly motivated to exploit it to the full. My parents were level-headed enough neither to nurture nor discourage my ambitions, which were no less than to compete for my county (then Leicestershire) and eventually for England. I well remember once sitting in the back seat of my father's car driving out of the Goodwood Bowling Club car park. We had just experienced a great family win — a mixed fours competition which included the three of us. I blithely mentioned that I had one

Jim Baker gives the benefit of his experience to Australian juniors

further ambition, which was to wear the English Rose on my blazer. There was a deadly hush from the front seat, and the subject was quickly changed. Your ambitions may be nothing like so grandiose, and you should tailor your approach to practising to your own goals.

Looking back on it, my game was very limited during those early years, and I am surprised that I did so well in competition play. I was almost completely reliant on the draw shot, which I suppose goes to show that if you can draw really close, consistently, you will never find yourself completely out of the running, even at county level.

After a few years of steady improvement, my game went through a somewhat troublesome transitional stage, which was inevitable. I realized that I would have to expand my repertoire, and by concentrating on the yard on, the various driving shots and so on I began to lose my earlier proficiency at the draw. There was no magic formula for recapturing it. It was only through a combination of practice and experience that I was able to assemble the game I now possess: more or less the complete range of accepted shots, with the draw as the cornerstone.

Why do I no longer practise, or at least practise so little that it might suggest a casual attitude to my performance? The answer is that I believe I would lose more than I would gain by doing so. I am dedicated to bowls, but my appetite for it is not unlimited. I spend a great deal of my time bowling as it is, and if I were to add hours of practice to my playing time I might become jaded. That is a very personal point of view. Most of the top bowlers practise regularly, and some of them do so rigorously. David Bryant views practice as an integral part of his craft, and I would be the last to argue with him. I merely do what I think is right for me.

Because I avoid practice, it might appear that I consider I have nothing more to learn about the game. That is emphatically not the case. I will never achieve absolute mastery of the game, technical or tactical, any more than anyone else has or will. I simply fear

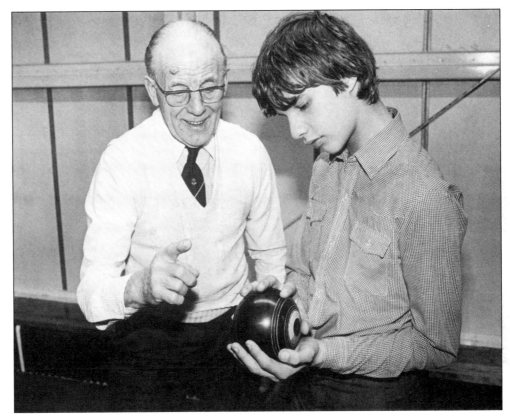

One of the first lessons for a novice is an explanation of the effects of bias

staleness more than I do rustiness. Moreover, there is one feature of my game that supports me in my unorthodox behaviour in this respect. My action, curious though that little flick of a delivery may appear, is entirely natural. I never give it a moment's thought, and I can truthfully say that during my career in top-flight competition I have never known it to fail me. I have not suffered the equivalent of the golfer's problem swing, or the snooker player's troublesome cue action, and therefore I have not been forced to re-examine my action in order to resolve a pressing difficulty. To say as much may be to give a hostage to fortune, but it is the fact of the

matter. I lose matches for a variety of reasons – the superior skill of my opponent on the day, lapses in concentration, tactical mistakes, too much or too little caution, indeed for all the reasons that you lose matches. Except for the one. I do not believe that I ever lose because my bowling technique has deserted me. If one day it does, whether tomorrow or a decade from now, then I will head straight for the practice green. Until then, I will go into my matches as fresh mentally and physically as I possibly can.

Concentration

Mental freshness is a great aid to concentration, and without keen concentration you will not get very far with bowls. Some find it more difficult than others to keep their minds wholly fixed on the task in hand for lengthy periods. It is not necessarily that they are less keen, less committed or less competitive, but simply that they have difficulty in keeping their thoughts from wandering. I can only tell you that sustained concentration, as total as the human mind will allow, is vital to success. In a contest between equals, the player with the more fiercely-concentrated willpower almost always emerges the winner.

I consider myself fortunate to have strong powers of concentration, and they have been sorely tested. I will give you an example that touches deeply on my personal feelings, but it makes the point more clearly than I could in any other way. In 1986 I was attempting to win the Gloucestershire Singles Championship, one of the few county titles that had eluded me despite repeated attempts since my arrival in that county in 1980. I had reached the semi-final stage, which is always of critical importance in these championships, because the top two from each county go through to contest the England title. Winning through to the final, therefore, is almost as significant as winning the championships. Nothing is more disheartening than to be knocked out in the semi-finals.

The match was set for six in the evening, and I was about to set off shortly after five when, at the last moment, I went back upstairs for

Noel Burrows, one of the game's best all-rounders, weighs up the situation. As with all sports, the ability to concentrate totally is a vital ingredient of successful bowling

anothor jumpor to ward off thc cvening chill. Because of that slight delay, I was still in the house when the phone rang. I answered it without hesitation. It might be good news, because my mother, who had undergone an operation in Leicestershire, was due for release from hospital that day. Perhaps it would be good luck wishes from home.

The reality was starkly different. The caller was a family friend, terribly upset about the fact that my mother had died that morning, and wishing to express his condolences. Then, as it became apparent from my stunned reaction that he was in fact breaking this terrible news to me, his grief became quite overwhelming. He simply had not realized that my father, knowing that it was very important to my mother that I win my match, had decided to grant me just a few more tranquil hours. Now, by accident, the scheme was in ruins.

I consoled our friend as well as I could, and told him to try to put our unfortunate conversation out of his mind, and that I would do the same. I then drove to the match, quite composed and with my thoughts riveted on the impending contest, played extremely well and won. Then I returned home and to the grief which had been temporarily suspended. I knew that I had done as my mother would have wished, and that she would have been proud of my performance, especially so because it was achieved under such trying circumstances.

Tony Allcock with his father Ernie and his late mother Joan. Both the Allcocks senior were very keen bowlers, and Tony inherited more than his fair share of talent

John Bell of England (left) is one of the steeliest competitors in the game – though nothing like so fearsome-looking away from the green

Playing under pressure

Concentration and self-discipline go a long way towards creating the ideal mental and emotional state for intense competition. That is the state of composure. To be composed is not the same thing as to be relaxed, much less laid back or indifferent. It is to be resolved, alert, attuned to the matter in hand, and in control of the complex processes whereby physical effort translates intelligent thought into constructive action. Anger, despair, fear of defeat and anticipation of victory – all of these quite normal reactions are the enemies of composure. Composure is of supreme importance at those very times when it is most difficult to maintain – under the most severe pressure. Of the many qualities that go into making a champion, the ability to cope with pressure is surely the most important. It is also the most elusive. If you really are an uncontrollable bundle of nerves, then nothing I can say will help you as you stand on the mat facing a shot that will determine the outcome of an important match. If you are one of the fortunate ones, whose adrenaline pushes you to new heights when it matters most, then you need no encouragement.

Having said that the ability to perform well under pressure is largely innate, I must emphasize that there is considerable scope for an individual to gain strength, or at least mask weakness, in this department. There are simple mental tricks you can conjure with in order to make a stressful situation appear more manageable. Take, for example, the daunting prospect of having to draw to the jack with your final bowl, with your

Martyn Davies is deep in thought as Ron Keating commences an end during the 1985 EBA semi-finals. You must try to remain composed, whatever the state of the match

opponent lying three. You will know from experience that, if roles were reversed and those three good bowls were yours, you would have every chance of drawing right in with the fourth – a pressure-free shot. As you prepare for the shot, therefore, imagine that those ominous opposition bowls are instead your own friendly counters, and play the draw accordingly. That may seem like childish self-deception, but it can work wonders.

A variation on this theme, still only relying on a simple act of the imagination, is to assume that your opponent will invariably deliver the perfect bowl. When he does, it will be no worse than you anticipated, and therefore it should not shake you unduly. When he achieves less than perfection, the situation can only be better than expected, and that should give you a fillip.

Aside from such relatively simple mental gymnastics, try not to increase the pressure by grappling with difficulties that are foreseeable, but only problematical. Suppose that at a critical stage your opponent's final bowl will leave you facing one of a number of tricky shots with yours. Depending upon what he decides to do, and how well he does it, you will, say, either have to play a yard on with your forehand, switch to the backhand for a perfect draw, or trail the jack through to your back bowl. It is completely pointless for you to wrack your fevered brain with these various scenarios, because what is certain is that you are only going to have to confront one of them. Try to relax, wait until you see his shot, and then address yourself to the real situation. Remember, too, that your opponent is under pressure just as you are. Whatever your inner turmoil, conceal it, and try to avoid the defeatist assumption that it will be you, rather than he, who will crack under the strain. Poker is not the only game that can reward calculated bluffing.

The worst sort of pressure you can fall victim to is pressure you create for yourself where the circumstances do not warrant it. It is the worst not because it is any more potentially destructive than any other form of pressure, but because it is completely unnecessary. There is enough inescapable pressure in competition without contriving it. Generally speaking I perform well under pressure, but I am not such a masochist as to court it – at least consciously!

Tony Allcock presents a perfect image of the determined, dedicated bowler. His concentration rarely falters, and it is this mental toughness as much as technical brilliance that makes him such a formidable competitor

Playing under pressure

During the 1986 World Indoor Championships, I found myself doing just that. I was playing against Noel Burrows the 1985 Superbowl Champion, and I was simply cruising along to what looked like an easy victory. I was leading by something like 18–3, and at that point, with the winning post in sight, Noel got the jack, changed the length and began to climb back by the odd shot. At around the 18–10 mark, it began to dawn on me that I had changed my game completely – that in fact control of the game had mysteriously shifted from me to Noel. In my keenness to close out the game, to reach that magic 21, I had become impetuous, pressing too hard, too early in each end, always looking for the one big shot that would see me home. Noel had shrewdly assessed this tactical waywardness, and was just quietly giving me enough rope to hang myself.

What I should have been doing, of course, with such a colossal lead, was just keeping the game tight, letting him take all the risks, and capitalizing on the inevitable mistakes he would make in doing so. Why on earth was I looking for some neck-or-nothing shot to win the game? As I struggled to regain control of the situation the score crept up to 18–16, and I was near to panic. The pressure was enormous, ludicrous though that struck me as I remembered the distant 18–3 margin that had melted so swiftly away. I had gone from looking ahead prematurely to victory to casting anxious glances over my shoulder at the spectre of defeat. In other words, I had stupidly got myself into a kind of time warp, where a tantaliz-

ing future had been overtaken by a remorseless past and I had to fight for dear life to get a grip on the present, which is where I should have been all along. Even at 18–16, there was no objective reason for the panic that threatened to engulf me. I have often felt quite sanguine going into a final end tied 20–all, content simply because I held final bowl. But to have squandered such a lead, to have heaped such pressure upon myself, to be on the brink of snatching defeat from the jaws of victory ...

In the event, I pulled myself together at the eleventh hour and struggled home the winner. I fervently hope that I have learned from that gruelling experience, and that you will be resolved to spare yourself the same.

Noel Burrows competing against Willie Wood at Superbowl '85, the scene of his greatest triumph. A year later, during the World Indoor Championships, Tony Allcock squandered a massive lead against Noel – and thereby put himself under enormous pressure

To succeed at the highest levels of the game it is essential to come to terms with fierce pressure – not least the pressure to perform well beneath the scrutiny of the TV eye

Tony Allcock proudly displaying his trophy for winning the World Indoor Singles title in 1987 – making it two years in succession. He is most fortunate in having a matchplay temperament quite equal to his bowling skills

Chapter 6 THE LAWS OF THE GAME

An understanding of the Laws of the Game is essential to its enjoyment. The situation with bowls is complicated by the fact that the various national associations are entitled to modify the code of laws set down by the International Bowling Board (IBB) in accordance with domestic conditions. What this means is that if you bowl in anything other than international competitions governed by the IBB, you will play according to national rules (outdoor or indoor). The World Indoor Bowls Council too stipulates its own rules. Nevertheless, all sets of rules are derived from the IBB Laws, which can be taken as the basis of the game wherever it is played. We thank the IBB for its kind permission in allowing us to reproduce the Laws of the Game.

Definitions

1. (a) *Controlling Body* means the body having immediate control of the conditions under which a match is played.

The order shall be:

(i) The International Bowling Board,

(ii) The National Bowling Association,

(iii) The State, Division, Local District or County Association,

(iv) The Club on whose Green the Match is played.

(b) *Skip* means the Player who, for the time being, is in charge of the head on behalf of the team.

(c) *Team* means either a four, triples or a pair.

(d) *Side* means any agreed number of Teams, whose combined scores determine the results of the match.

(e) *Four* means a team of four players whose positions in order of playing are named Lead, Second, Third, Skip.

(f) *Bowl in Course* means a bowl from the time of its delivery until it comes to rest.

(g) *End* means the playing of the Jack and all the bowls of all the opponents in the same direction on a rink.

(h) *Head* means the Jack and such bowls as have come to rest within the boundary of the rink and are not dead.

(i) *Mat Line* means the edge of the Mat which is nearest to the front ditch. From the centre of the Mat Line all necessary measurements to Jack or bowls shall be taken.

(j) *Master Bowl* means a bowl which has been approved by the IBB as having the minimum bias required, as well as in all other respects complying with the Laws of the Game and is engraved with the words *Master Bowl*.

(i) A Standard Bowl of the same bias as the Master Bowl shall be kept in the custody of each National Association.

(ii) A Standard Bowl shall be provided for the use of each official Licensed Tester.

Tony Allcock uses the regulation six-foot measure to ensure that the mat is correctly positioned in relation to the ditch

(k) *Jack High* means that the nearest portion of the Bowl referred to is in line with and at the same distance from the Mat Line as the nearest portion of the Jack.

(l) *Pace of Green* means the number of seconds taken by a bowl from the time of its delivery to the moment it comes to rest, approximately 30 yards (27.43 metres) from the Mat Line.

(m) *Displaced* as applied to a Jack or Bowl means *disturbed* by any agency that is not sanctioned by these laws.

(n) *A set of bowls* means four bowls all of which are the same manufacture and are of the same size, weight, colour and serial number where applicable.

The Green

2. The Green – Area and Surface
The Green should form a square of not less than 40 yards (36.58 metres) and not more than 44 yards (40.23 metres) a side. It shall have a suitable playing surface which shall be level. It shall be provided with suitable boundaries in the form of a ditch and bank.

3. The Ditch
The Green shall be surrounded by a ditch which shall have a holding surface not injurious to bowls and be free from obstacles. The ditch shall be not less than 8 inches (203mm) nor more than 15 inches (381mm) wide and it shall be not less than 2 inches (51mm) nor more than 8 inches (203mm) below the level of the green.

4. Banks
The bank shall be not less than 9 inches (229mm) above the level of the green, preferably upright, or alternatively at an angle of not more than 35 degrees from the perpendicular. The surface of the face of the bank shall be non-injurious to bowls. No steps likely to interfere with play shall be cut in the banks.

5. Division of the Green
The Green shall be divided into spaces called rinks, each not more than 19 feet (5.79 metres), nor less than 18 feet (5.48 metres), wide. They shall be numbered consecutively, the centre line of each rink being marked on the bank at each end by a wooden peg or other suitable device. The four corners of the rinks shall be marked by pegs made of wood, or other suitable material, painted white and fixed to the face of the bank and flush therewith or alternatively fixed on the bank not more than 4 inches (102mm) back from the face thereof. The corner pegs shall be connected by a green thread drawn tightly along the surface of the green, with sufficient loose thread to reach the corres-

A view of the World Championships held in Aberdeen in 1984, showing the rinks properly marked off

ponding pegs on the face or surface of the bank, in order to define the boundary of the rink.

White pegs or discs shall be fixed on the side banks to indicate a clear distance of 76 feet (23.16 metres) from the ditch on the line of play. Under no circumstances shall the boundary thread be lifted while the bowl is in motion. The boundary pegs of an outside rink shall be placed at least 2 feet (61cm) from the side ditch.

6. Permissible Variations of Laws 2 and 5

(a) National Associations may admit Greens in the form of a square not longer than 44 yards (40.23 metres), nor shorter than 33 yards (30.17 metres), or of a rectangle of which the longer side should not be more than 44 yards (40.23 metres) and the shorter side not less than 33 yards (30.17 metres).

(b) For domestic play the Green may be divided into Rinks, not less than 14 feet (4.27 metres) nor more than 19 feet (5.79 metres) wide. National Associations may dispense with the use of boundary threads.

Mat, Jack, Bowls, Footwear

7. Mat
The Mat shall be of a definite size, namely 24 inches (61cm) long and 14 inches (35.6cm) wide.

8. Jack
The Jack shall be round and white, with a diameter of not less than $2\frac{15}{32}$ inches (63mm), nor more than $2\frac{17}{32}$ inches (64mm), and not less than 8 ounces (227g), nor more than 10 ounces (283g) in weight.

9. Bowls
(a) (i) Bowls shall be made of wood, rubber or composition and shall be black or brown in colour, and each bowl of the set shall bear the member's individual and distinguishing mark on each side. The provision relating to the distinguishing mark on each side of the bowl need not apply other than in International

Former IBB Secretary David Marshall (left) and IBB President Garnett Putland display the two specimen bowls from which the Master Bowl was selected in 1987. Both perfect examples of the modern bowl, maybe, but Garnett Putland's won

Matches, World Bowls Championships and Commonwealth Games.

Bowls made of wood (lignum vitae) shall have a maximum diameter of $5\frac{1}{4}$ inches (133.35mm) and a minimum diameter of $4\frac{5}{8}$ inches (117mm) and the weight shall not exceed 3lb 8oz (1.59kg). Loading of bowls made of wood is strictly prohibited.

(ii) For all International and Commonwealth Games Matches, a bowl made of rubber or composition shall have a maximum diameter of $5\frac{1}{8}$ inches (130mm) and a minimum diameter of $4\frac{5}{8}$ inches (117mm) and the weight shall not exceed 3lb 8oz (1.59kg).

Subject to bowls bearing a current stamp of the Board and/or a current stamp of a Member National Author-

ity and/or the current stamp of the BIBC and provided they comply with the Board's Laws, they may be used in all matches controlled by the Board or by any Member National Authority.

Notwithstanding the aforegoing provisions, any Member National Authority may adopt a different scale of weights and sizes of bowls to be used in matches under its own control – such bowls may not be validly used in International Matches, World Championships, Commonwealth Games or other matches controlled by the Board if they differ from the Board's Laws, and unless stamped with a current stamp of the Board or any Member National Authority or the BIBC.

(iii) The controlling body may, at its discretion, supply and require players to temporarily affix an adhesive marking to their bowls in any competition game. Any temporary marking under this Law shall be regarded as part of the bowl for all purposes under these Laws.

(b) Bias of Bowls

The Master Bowl shall have a Bias approved by the International Bowling Board. A Bowl shall have a Bias not less than that of the Master Bowl, and shall bear the imprint of the Stamp of the International Bowling Board, or that of its National Association. National Associations may adopt a standard which exceeds the bias of the Master Bowl. To ensure accuracy of bias and visibility of stamp, all bowls shall be re-tested and re-stamped at least once every ten years, or earlier if the date of the stamp is not clearly legible.

(c) Objection to Bowls

A challenge may be lodged by an Opposing Player and/or by the Official Umpire and/or the Controlling Body.

A challenge or any intimation thereof shall not be lodged with any opposing player during the progress of a Match.

A challenge may be lodged with the Umpire at any time during a Match, provided the Umpire is not a Player in that or any other match of the same competition.

If a challenge be lodged it shall be made not later than ten minutes after the completion of the final end in which the Bowl was used.

Once a challenge is lodged with the Umpire, it cannot be withdrawn.

The challenge shall be based on the grounds that the bowl does not comply with one or more of the requirements set out in Law 9(a) and 9(b).

The Umpire shall request the user of the bowl to surrender it to him for forwarding to the Controlling Body. If the owner of the challenged bowl refuses to surrender it to the Umpire, the Match shall thereupon be forfeited to the opponent. The user or owner, or both, may be disqualified from playing in any match controlled or permitted by the Controlling Body, so long as the bowl remains untested by a licensed tester.

On receipt of the fee and the bowl, the Umpire shall take immediate steps to hand them to the Secretary of the Controlling Body, who shall arrange for a table test to be made as soon as practicable, and in the presence of a representative of the Controlling Body.

If a table test be not readily available, and any delay would unduly interfere with the progress of the competition, then, should an approved green testing device be available, it may be used to make an immediate test on the Green. If a green test be made it shall be done by,

or in the presence of, the Umpire over a distance of not less than 70 feet (21.35 metres). The comparison shall be between the challenged bowl and a standard bowl, or if it be not readily available then a recently stamped bowl, of similar size or nearly so, should be used.

The decision of the Umpire, as a result of the test, shall be final and binding for that match.

The result of the subsequent table test shall not invalidate the decision given by the Umpire on the green test.

If a challenged bowl, after an official table test, be found to comply with all the requirements of Law 9(a) and (b), it shall be returned to the user or owner and the fee paid by the challenger shall be forfeited to the Controlling Body.

If the challenged bowl be found not to comply with Law 9(a) and (b), the match in which it was played shall be forfeited to the opponent, and the fee paid by the challenger shall be returned to him.

If a bowl in the hands of a licensed tester has been declared as not complying with Law 9(a) and (b), by an official representative of the Controlling Body, then, with the consent of the owner, and at his expense, it shall be altered so as to comply before being returned to him.

If the owner refuses his consent, and demands the return of his bowl, any current official stamp appearing thereon shall be cancelled prior to its return.

(d) Alteration to Bias

A player shall not alter, or cause to be altered, other than by an official bowl tester, the bias of any bowl, bearing the imprint of the official stamp of the Board, under penalty of suspension from playing for a period to be determined by the Council of the National Association, of which his club is a member. Such suspension shall be subject to confirmation by the Board, or a committee thereof appointed for that purpose, and shall be operative among all associations in membership with the Board.

10. Footwear

Players, Umpires and Markers shall wear white, brown or black smooth-soled heel-less footwear while playing on the green or acting as Umpires or Markers.

Arranging a game

11. General form and duration

A game of bowls shall be played on one rink or on several rinks. It shall consist of a specified number of shots or ends, or shall be played for any period of time as previously arranged.

The ends of the game shall be played alternately in opposite directions excepting as provided in Laws 38, 42, 44, 46 and 47.

12. Selecting the rinks for play

When a match is to be played, the draw for the rinks to be played on shall be made by the skips or their representatives.

In a match for a trophy or where competing skips have previously been drawn, the draw to decide the numbers of the rinks to be played on

shall be made by the visiting skips or their representatives.

No player in a competition or match shall play on the same rink on the day of such competition or match before play commences under penalty of disqualification.

This law shall not apply in the case of open Tournaments.

13. Play arrangements

Games shall be organized in the following play arrangements:
(a) As a single game.
(b) As a team game.
(c) As a sides game.
(d) As a series of single games, team games, or side games.
(e) As a special tournament of games:

14. A single game shall be played

Brown shoes it must be, according to EBA rules, but in IBB tournaments (the principal television fare) white shoes are permitted

on one rink of a Green as a single-handed game by two contending players, each playing two, three or four bowls singly and alternately.

15. (a) A pairs game by two contending teams of two players called lead and skip according to the order in which they play, and who at each end shall play four bowls alternately, the leads first, then the skips similarly.

(For other than International and Commonwealth Games, players in a pairs game may play two, three or four bowls each, as previously arranged by the Controlling Body.)

(b) A pairs game by two contending teams of two players called Lead and Skip according to the order in which they play, and who at each end shall play four bowls and may play alternatively in the following order: Lead 2 bowls, Skip 2 bowls, then repeat this order of play.

16. A triples game by two contending teams of three players, who shall play two or three bowls singly and in turn, the leads playing first.

17. A fours game by two contending teams of four players, each member playing two bowls singly and in turn.

18. A side game shall be played by two contending sides, each composed of an equal number of teams/players.

19. Games in series shall be arranged to be played on several and consecutive occasions as:

(a) A series or sequence of games organized in the form of an eliminating competition, and arranged as singles, pairs, triples or fours.

(b) A series or sequence of side matches organized in the form of a league competition, or an eliminating competition, or of inter-association matches.

20. A special tournament of games

Single games and team games may also be arranged in group form as a special tournament of games in which the contestants play each other in turn, or they may play as paired-off teams of players on one or several greens in accordance with a common

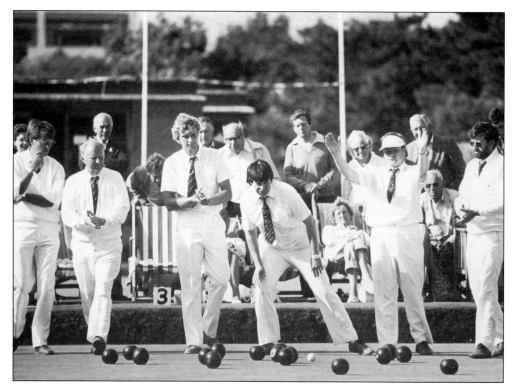

time-table, success being adjudged by the number of games won, or by the highest net score in shots in accordance with the regulations governing the Tournament.

21. For International Matches, World Bowls and Commonwealth Games, in matches where played,
(i) Singles shall be 25 shots up (shots in excess of 25 shall not count), four bowls each player, played alternately;
(ii) Pairs shall be 21 ends, four bowls each player, played alternately;
(iii) Triples shall be 18 ends, three bowls each player, played alternately;
(iv) Fours shall be 21 ends, two bowls each player, played alternately;

The fours game is the backbone of bowls, not least because it makes the most efficient use of available facilities

PROVIDED that pairs, triples and fours may be of a lesser number of ends, but in the case of pairs and fours there shall not be less than 18 ends and in the case of triples not less than 15 ends, subject in all cases to the express approval of the Board as represented by its most senior officer present. If there be no officer of the Board present at the time, the decision shall rest with the *Controlling Body* as defined in Law 1. Any decision to curtail the number of ends to be played shall be made before the commencement of any game, and such decision shall only be made on the grounds of climatic conditions, inclement weather or shortage of time to complete a programme.

22. Awards

Cancelled; see By-Laws after Rule 73 under heading 'Professional Bowler'.

Starting the game

23. (a) Trial ends

Before start of play in any competition, match or game, or on the resumption of an unfinished competition, match or game on another day, not more than one trial end each way shall be played.

(b) Tossing for opening play

The captains in a side game or skips in a team shall toss to decide which side or team shall play first, but in all singles games the opponents shall toss, the winner of the toss to have the option of decision. In the event of a tied (no score) or a dead end, the first to play in the tied end or dead end shall again play first.

In all ends subsequent to the first the winner of the preceding scoring end shall play first.

24. Placing the Mat

At the beginning of the first end the player to play first shall place the mat lengthwise on the centre line of the rink, the front edge of the mat to be 6 feet (1.84 metres) from the ditch. (Where ground sheets are in use, the mat at the first and every subsequent end, shall be placed at the back edge

More than a little anxious to get on with it, Dennis Katunarich almost rips the mat from beneath Peter Belliss's feet as he delivers his final bowl in the 1985 Gateway Masters

of the sheet – the mat's front edge being 6 feet (1.84 metres) from the ditch.)

25. The Mat and its replacement

After play has commenced in any end the mat shall not be moved from its first position.

If the mat be displaced during the progress of an end it shall be replaced as near as practicable in the same position.

If the mat be out of alignment with the centre line of the rink it may be straightened at any time during the end.

After the last bowl in each end has come to rest in play, or has sooner become dead, the mat shall be lifted and placed wholly beyond the face of the rear bank. Should the mat be picked up by a player before the end has been completed, the opposing player shall have the right of replacing the mat in its original position.

26. The Mat in subsequent ends

(a) In all subsequent ends the front edge of the mat shall be not less than 6 feet (1.84 metres) from the rear ditch and the front edge of the mat not less than 76 feet (23.16 metres) from the front ditch and on the centre line of the rink of play.

(b) Should the Jack be improperly delivered under Law 30, the opposing player may then move the mat in the line of play, subject to Clause (a) above and deliver the Jack, but shall not play first. Should the Jack be improperly delivered twice by each player in any end, it shall not be delivered again in that end, but shall be centred so that the front of the Jack is a distance of 6 feet (1.84 metres) from the opposite ditch, and the mat placed at the option of the first to play.

If after the Jack is set at regulation length from the ditch (6 feet or 1.84 metres), both players each having improperly delivered the Jack twice, the end is made Dead, the winner of the preceding scoring end shall deliver the Jack when the end is played anew.

27. Stance on Mat

A player shall take his stance on the mat, and, at the moment of delivering the Jack or his Bowl, shall have one foot remaining entirely within the confines of the mat. The foot may be either in contact with, or over, the mat. Failure to observe this law constitutes foot-faulting.

28. Foot-faulting

Should a player infringe the Law of foot-faulting the Umpire may, after having given a warning, have the bowl stopped and declared dead. If the bowl has disturbed the head, the opponent shall have the option of either resetting the head, leaving the head as altered or declaring the end dead.

29. Delivering the Jack

The Player to play first shall deliver the Jack. If the Jack in its original course comes to rest at a distance of less than 2 yards (1.84 metres) from the opposite ditch, it shall be moved out to a mark at that distance so that the front of the jack is 6 feet (1.84 metres) from the front ditch.

If the Jack during its original course be obstructed or deflected by a neutral object or neutral person, or by a marker, opponent, or member of the opposing team, it shall be re-delivered by the same player. If it be obstructed or deflected by a member of his own team, it shall be re-delivered by the lead of the opposing team, who shall be entitled to reset the mat.

30. Jack improperly delivered

Should the Jack in any end be not delivered from a proper stance on the mat, or if it ends its original course in the ditch or outside the side boundary of the rink, or less than 70 feet (21.35 metres) in a straight line of play from

Jean Valls of Surrey has, correctly, one foot entirely within the confines of the mat at the moment of delivery

the front edge of the mat, it shall be returned and the opposing player shall deliver the Jack, but shall not play first.

The Jack shall be returned if it is improperly delivered, but the right of the player first delivering the Jack in that end, to play the first bowl of the end shall not be affected.

No player shall be permitted to challenge the legality of the original length of the Jack after each player in a singles game or leads in a team game have each bowled one bowl.

31. Variations to Laws 24, 26, 29 and 30

Notwithstanding anything contained in Laws 24, 26, 29 and 30, any

National Authority may for domestic purposes, but not in any International Matches, World Bowls Championships or Commonwealth Games, vary any of the distances mentioned in these Laws.

Movement of bowls

32. Live Bowl

A Bowl which, in its original course on the Green, comes to rest within the boundaries of the rink, and not less than 15 yards (13.71 metres) from the front edge of the mat, shall be accounted as a *Live* bowl and shall be in play.

33. Touchers

A bowl which, in its original course on the green, touches the Jack, even though such bowl passes into the ditch within the boundaries of the rink, shall be counted as a *live* bowl and shall be called a *toucher*. If after having come to rest a bowl falls over and touches the Jack before the next succeeding bowl is delivered, or if in the case of the last bowl of an end it falls and touches the Jack within the period of half-minute invoked under Law 53, such bowl shall also be a *toucher*. No bowl shall be accounted a *toucher* by playing on to, or by coming into contact with, the Jack while the Jack is in the ditch. If a *toucher* in the ditch cannot be seen from the mat its position may be marked by a white or coloured peg about 2 inches (51mm) broad placed upright on the top of the bank and immediately in line with the place where the *toucher* rests.

34. Marking a Toucher

A *toucher* shall be clearly marked with a chalk mark by a member of the player's team. If, in the opinion of either Skip, or opponent in Singles, a *toucher* or a wrongly chalked bowl comes to rest in such a position that the act of making a chalk mark, or of erasing it, is likely to move the bowl or to alter the head, the bowl shall not be marked or have its mark erased but shall be *indicated* as a *toucher* or *non-toucher* as the case may be. If a bowl is not so marked or not so *indicated* before the succeeding bowl comes to rest it ceases to be a *toucher*. If both Skips or opponents agree that any subsequent movement of the bowl eliminates the necessity for continuation of the *indicated* provision the bowl shall thereupon be marked or have the chalk mark erased as the case may be. Care should be taken to remove *toucher* marks from all bowls before they are played, but should a player fail to do so, and should the bowl not become a *toucher* in the end in play, the marks shall be removed by the opposing Skip or his deputy or marker immediately the bowl comes to rest unless the bowl is *indicated* as a *non-toucher* in circumstances governed by earlier provisions of this Law.

35. Movement of Touchers

A *toucher* in play in the ditch may be moved by the impact of a jack in play or of another *toucher* in play, and also by the impact of a non-toucher which remains in play after the impact, and any movement of the *toucher* by such incidents shall be valid. However, should the non-toucher enter the ditch at any time after the impact, it shall be dead, and the *toucher* shall be deemed to have been displaced by a dead bowl and the provisions of Law 38(e) shall apply.

36. Bowl Accounted Dead

(a) Without limiting the application of any other of these Laws, a bowl shall be accounted dead if it:

(i) not being a *toucher*, comes to rest in the ditch or rebounds on to the playing surface of the rink after contact with the bank or with the Jack or a *toucher* in the ditch, or

(ii) after completing its original course, or after being moved as a result of play, it comes to rest wholly outside the boundaries of the playing surface of the rink, or within 15 yards (13.71 metres) of the front of the mat, or

(iii) in its original course, pass beyond a side boundary of the rink on a bias which would prevent its re-entering the rink. (A bowl is not rendered *dead* by a player carrying it

A toucher must be clearly marked with chalk by a member of the player's team or the marker

whilst inspecting the head.)

(b) Skips, or Opponents in Singles, shall agree on the question as to whether or not a bowl is *dead*, and, having reached agreement, the question shall not later be subject to appeal to the Umpire. Any member of either team may request a decision from the Skips but no member shall remove any bowl prior to the agreement of the Skips. If Skips or Opponents are unable to reach agreement as to whether or not a bowl is *dead* the matter shall be referred to the Umpire.

37. Bowl Rebounding

Only *Touchers* rebounding from the face of the bank to the ditch or to the rink shall remain in play.

38. Bowl displacement

(a) Displacement by rebounding *non-toucher* – bowl displaced by a *non-toucher* rebounding from the bank shall be restored as near as possible to its original position by a member of the opposing team.

(b) Displacement by participating player – if a bowl, while in motion or at rest on the green, or a *toucher* in the ditch, be interfered with, or displaced by one of the players, the opposing skip shall have the option of:
(i) restoring the bowl as near as possible to its original position;
(ii) letting it remain where it rests;
(iii) declaring the bowl *dead*;
(iv) or declaring the end dead.

(c) Displacement by a neutral object or neutral person (other than as provided in Clause (d) hereof):
(i) of a bowl in its original course – if such a bowl be displaced within the boundaries of the rink of play without

having disturbed the head, it shall be replayed. If it be displaced and it has disturbed the head, the skips, or the opponents in singles, shall reach agreement on the final position of the displaced bowl and on the replacement of the head, otherwise the end shall be dead. These provisions shall also apply to a bowl in its original course displaced outside the boundaries of the rink of play provided such bowl was running on a bias which would have enabled it to re-enter the rink.

(ii) of a bowl at rest, or in motion as a result of play after being at rest – if such a bowl be displaced, the skips, or opponents in singles, shall come to an agreement as to the position of the bowl and of the replacement of any part of the head disturbed by the displaced bowl, otherwise the end shall be dead.

(d) Displacement inadvertently produced – if a bowl be moved at the time of it being marked or measured it shall be restored to its former position by an opponent. If such displacement is caused by a Marker or an Umpire, the Marker or Umpire shall replace the bowl.

(e) Displacement by dead bowl – if a *toucher* in the ditch be displaced by a dead bowl from the rink of play, it shall be restored to its original position by a player of the opposite team or by the marker.

39. Line Bowls

A bowl shall not be accounted as outside any circle or line unless it be entirely clear of it. This shall be ascertained by looking perpendicularly down upon the bowl or by placing a square on the green.

Movement of Jack

40. A Live Jack in the Ditch

A Jack moved by a bowl in play into the front ditch within the boundaries of the rink shall be deemed to be *live*. It may be moved by the impact of a *toucher* in play and also by the impact of a *non-toucher* which remains in play after the impact, any movement of the Jack by such incidents shall be valid. However, should the *non-toucher* enter the ditch after impact, it shall be *dead* and the Jack shall be deemed to have been *displaced* by a *dead* bowl and the provisions of Law 48 shall apply. If the Jack in the ditch cannot be seen from the mat its position shall be marked by a *white* peg about 2 inches (51mm) broad and not more than 4 inches (102mm) in height, placed upright on top of the bank and immediately in line from the place where the Jack rests.

41. A Jack accounted dead

Should the Jack be driven by a Bowl in play and come to rest wholly beyond the boundary of the rink, i.e. over the bank, or over the side boundary, or into any opening or inequality of any kind in the bank, or rebound to a distance of less than 61 feet (18.59 metres) in direct line from the centre of the front edge of the mat to the Jack in its rebounded position, it shall be accounted *dead*.

('National Associations have the option to vary the distance to which a Jack may rebound and still be playable for games other than International and Commonwealth Games.')

42. Dead End

When the Jack is *dead* the end shall be regarded as a *dead* end and shall not be accounted as a played end even though all the bowls in that end have been played. All *dead* ends shall be played anew in the same direction unless both Skips or Opponents in Singles agree to play in the opposite direction.

After a *dead* end situation the right to deliver the Jack shall always return to the player who delivered the original Jack.

43. Playing to a boundary Jack

The Jack, if driven to the side boundary of the rink and not wholly beyond its limits, may be played to on either hand and, if necessary, a bowl may pass outside the side limits of the rink. A bowl so played, which comes to rest within the boundaries of the rink, shall not be accounted *dead*.

If the Jack be driven to the side boundary line and comes to rest partly within the limits of the rink, a bowl played outside the limits of the rink and coming to rest entirely outside the boundary line, even though it has made contact with the jack, shall be accounted *dead* and shall be removed to the bank by a member of the player's team.

44. A Damaged Jack

In the event of a jack being damaged, the Umpire shall decide if another jack is necessary and, if so, the end shall be regarded as a *dead* end and another jack shall be substi-

A jack driven to ditch within the rink boundaries is 'live'

tuted and the end shall be replayed anew.

45. A rebounding Jack

If the jack is driven against the face of the bank and rebounds on to the rink, or after being played into the ditch, it be operated on by a *toucher*, so as to find its way on to the rink, it shall be played to in the same manner as if it had never left the rink.

46. Jack displacement

(a) By a player

If the jack be diverted from its course while in motion on the green, or displaced while at rest on the green, or in the ditch, by any one of the players, the opposing skip shall have the jack restored to its former position, or allow it to remain where it rests and play the end to a finish, or declare the end

dead.

(b) Inadvertently produced

If the jack be moved at the time of measuring by a player it shall be restored to its former position by an opponent.

47. Jack displaced by non-player

(a) If the jack, whether in motion or at rest on the rink, or in the ditch, be displaced by a bowl from another rink, or by any object or by an individual not a member of the team, the two skips shall decide as to its original position, and if they are unable to agree, the end shall be declared *dead*.

(b) If a jack be displaced by a marker or umpire it shall be restored by him to its original position of which he shall be the sole judge.

48. Jack displaced by non-toucher

A jack displaced in the rink of play by a *non-toucher* rebounding from the bank shall be restored, or as near as possible, to its original position by a player of the opposing team. Should a jack, however, after having been played into the ditch, be displaced by a *dead bowl* it shall be restored to its marked position by a player of the opposing side or by the marker.

Fours play

The basis of the Game of Bowls is Fours Play

49. The rink and fours play

(a) Designation of players. A team shall consist of four players, named respectively lead, second, third and skip, according to the order in which they play, each playing two bowls.

(b) Order of Play. The leads shall play their two bowls alternately, and so on, each pair of players in succession to the end. No one shall play until his opponent's bowl shall have come to rest. Except under circumstances provided for in Law 63, the order of play shall not be changed after the first end has been played, under penalty of disqualification, such penalty involving the forfeiture of the match or game to the opposing team.

50. Possession of the Rink

Possession of the rink shall belong to the team whose bowl is being played. The players in possession of the rink for the time being shall not be interfered with, annoyed, or have their attention distracted in any way by their opponents.

As soon as each bowl shall have come to rest, possession of the rink shall be transferred to the other team, time being allowed for marking a *toucher*.

51. Position of Players

Players of each team not in the act of playing or controlling play shall stand behind the jack and away from the head, or one yard (92cm) behind the mat. As soon as the bowl is delivered, the skip or player directing, if in front of the jack, shall retire behind it.

52. Players and their duties

(a) The Skip shall have sole charge of his team, and his instructions shall be observed by his players.

With the opposing skip he shall decide all disputed points, and when both agree their decision shall be final.

If both skips cannot agree, the point in dispute shall be referred to, and considered by, an Umpire whose decision shall be final.

A skip may at any time delegate his powers and any of his duties to other members of his team provided that such delegation is notified to the opposing skip.

(b) The third. The third player may have deputed to him the duty of measuring any and all disputed shots.

(c) The second. The second player shall keep a record of all shots scored for and against his team and shall at all times retain possession of the score card whilst play is in progress. He shall see that the names of all players are entered on the score card; shall compare his record of the game with that of the opposing second player as each end is declared, and at the close of the game shall hand his score card to his skip.

(d) The Lead. The Lead shall place the mat, and shall deliver the jack ensuring that the jack is properly centred before playing his first bowl.

(e) In addition to the duties specified in the preceding clauses, any player may undertake such duties as may be assigned to him by the skip in Clause 52(a) hereof.

Result of end

53. The shot

A shot or shots shall be adjudged by the bowl or bowls nearer to the jack than any bowl played by the opposing player or players.

When the last bowl has come to rest, half a minute shall elapse, if either team desires, before the shots are counted.

Neither jack nor bowls shall be moved until each skip has agreed to the number of shots, except in circumstances where a bowl has to be moved to allow the measuring of another bowl.

54. Measuring conditions to be observed

No measuring shall be allowed until the end has been completed.

All measurements shall be made to the nearest point of each object. If a bowl requiring to be measured is resting on another bowl which prevents its measurement, the best available means shall be taken to secure its position, whereupon the other bowl shall be removed. The same course shall be followed where more than two bowls are involved, or where, in the course of measuring, a single bowl is in danger of falling or otherwise changing its position.

When it is necessary to measure to a bowl or jack in the ditch, and another bowl or jack on the green, the measurement shall be made with the ordinary flexible measure. Calipers may be used to determine the shot only when the bowls in question and the jack are on the same plane.

55. Tie – No shot

When at the conclusion of play in any end the nearest bowl of each team is touching the jack, or is deemed to be equidistant from the jack, there shall be no score recorded. The end shall be declared *drawn* and shall be counted a played end.

56. Nothing in these Laws shall be deemed to make it mandatory for the last player to play his last bowl in any end, but he shall declare to his opponent or opposing skip his intention to refrain from playing it before the commencement of determining the result of the end and this declaration shall be irrevocable.

Game decisions

57. Games played on one occasion

In the case of a single game or a team game or a side game played on one occasion, or at any stage of an eliminating competition, the victory decision shall be awarded to the player, team, or side of players producing at the end of the game, the higher total score of shots, or in the case of a 'game of winning ends' a

All measurements are made to the nearest points of the two objects

majority of winning ends.

58. Tournament games and games in series

In the case of Tournament games or games in series, the victory decision shall be awarded to the player, team or side of players producing at the end of the tournament or series of contests, either the largest number of winning games or the highest net score of shots in accordance with the regulations governing the tournament or series of games.

Points may be used to indicate game successes.

Where points are equal, the aggregate shots scored against each team (or side) shall be divided into the aggregate shots it has scored. The team (or side) with the highest result shall be declared the winner.

59. Playing to a finish and possible drawn games

If in an eliminating competition, consisting of a stated or agreed upon number of ends, it be found, when all the ends have been played, that the scores are equal, an extra end or ends shall be played until a decision has been reached.

The captains or skips shall toss and the winner shall have the right to decide who shall play first. The extra end shall be played from where the previous end was completed, and the mat shall be placed in accordance with Law 24.

Defaults of players in fours play

60. Absentee players in any team or side

(a) **In a single fours game,** for a trophy, prize or other competitive award, where a club is represented by only one four, each member of such four shall be a bona fide member of the club. Unless all four players appear and are ready to play at the end of the maximum waiting period of 30 minutes, or should they introduce an ineligible player, then that team shall forfeit the match to the opposing team.

(b) **In a domestic fours game.** Where, in a domestic fours game the number of players cannot be accommodated in full teams of four players, three players may play against three players, but shall suffer the deduction of one-fourth of the total score of each team.

A smaller number of players than

six shall be excluded from that game.

(c) **In a Side game.** If within a period of 30 minutes from the time fixed for the game, a single player is absent from one or both teams in a side game, whether a friendly club match or a match for a trophy, prize or other award, the game shall proceed, but in the defaulting team, the number of bowls shall be made up by the lead and second players playing three bowls each, but one-fourth of the total shots scored by each *four* playing three men shall be deducted from their score at the end of the game.

Fractions shall be taken into account.

(d) **In a Side game.** Should such default take place where more fours than one are concerned, or where a four has been disqualified for some other infringement, and where the average score is to decide the contest, the scores of the non-defaulting fours only shall be counted, but such average shall, as a penalty in the case of the defaulting side, be arrived at by dividing the aggregate score of that side by the number of fours that should have been played and not as in the case of the other side, by the number actually engaged in the game.

61. Play irregularities
(a) **Playing out of turn.** When a player has played before his turn the opposing skip shall have the right to stop the bowl in its course and it shall be played in its proper turn, but in the event of the bowl so played, having moved or displaced the jack or bowl, the opposing skip shall have the option of allowing the end to remain as it is after the bowl so played, has come to rest, or having the end declared *dead*.

(b) **Playing the wrong bowl.** A bowl played by mistake shall be replaced by the player's own bowl.

(c) **Changing bowls.** A player shall not be allowed to change his bowls during the course of a game, or in a resumed game, unless they be objected to, as provided in Law 9(c), or when a bowl has been so damaged in the course of play as, in the opinion of the Umpire, to render the bowl (or bowls) unfit for play.

(d) **Omitting to play**
(i) If the result of an end has been agreed upon, or the head has been touched in the agreed process of determining the result, then a player who forfeits or has omitted to play a bowl, shall forfeit the right to play it.

(ii) A player who has neglected to play a bowl in the proper sequence shall forfeit the right to play such bowl, if a bowl has been played by each team before such mistake was discovered.

(iii) If before the mistake be noticed, a bowl has been delivered in the reversed order and the head has not been disturbed, the opponent shall then play two successive bowls to restore the correct sequence.

If the head has been disturbed Clause 61(a) shall apply.

62. Play Interruptions
(a) **Game Stoppages.** When a game of any kind is stopped, either by mutual arrangement or by the Umpire, after appeal to him on account of darkness or the conditions of the weather, or any other valid reason, it shall be resumed with the scores as they were when the game stopped. An end commenced, but not completed, shall be declared null.

(b) **Substitutes in a resumed game.** If in a resumed game any one of the four original players be not available, one substitute shall be permitted as stated in Law 63 below. Players, however, shall not be transferred from one team to another.

Influences affecting play

63. Leaving the Green
If during the course of a side fours, triples or pairs game a player has to leave the green owing to illness, or other reasonable cause, his place shall be filled by a substitute, if in the opinion of both skips (or failing agreement by them, then in the opinion of the Controlling Body) such substitution is necessary. Should the player affected be a skip, his duties and position in a fours game shall be assumed by the third player, and the substitute shall play either as a lead, second or third. In the case of Triples the substitute may play either as lead or second but not as skip and in the case of Pairs the substitute shall play as lead only. Such substitute shall be a member of the club to which the team belongs. In domestic play National Associations may decide the position of any substitute.

If during the course of a single-handed game, a player has to leave the green owing to illness, or reasonable cause, the provision of Law 62(a) shall be observed.

No player shall be allowed to delay the play by leaving the rink or team, unless with the consent of his opponent, and then only for a period not exceeding ten minutes.

Contravention of this Law shall entitle the opponent or opposing team to claim the game or match.

64. Objects on the Green

Under no circumstances, other than as provided in Laws 29, 33 and 40, shall any extraneous object to assist a player be placed on the green, or on the bank, or on the jack, or on a bowl or elsewhere.

65. Unforeseen incidents

If, during the course of play, the position of the jack or bowls be disturbed by wind, storm, or by any neutral object the end shall be declared *dead*, unless the skips are agreed as to the replacement of jack or bowls.

Domestic arrangements

66. In addition to any matters specifically mentioned in these Laws, National Associations may, in circumstances dictated by climate or other local conditions, make such other regulations as are deemed necessary and desirable, but such regulations must be submitted to the IBB for approval. For this purpose the Board shall appoint a Committee to be known as the *Laws Committee* with powers to grant approval or otherwise to any proposal, such decision being valid until the proposal is submitted to the Board for a final decision.

Spectators must do nothing whatever to disturb the players

67. Local Arrangements

Constituent clubs of National Associations shall also in making their domestic arrangements make such regulations as are deemed necessary to govern their club competitions, but such regulations shall comply with the Laws of the Game, and be approved by the Council of their National Association.

68. National Visiting Teams or Sides

No team or side of bowlers visiting overseas or the British Isles shall be recognized by the International Bowling Board unless it first be sanctioned and recommended by the National Association to which its members are affiliated.

69. Contracting out

No club or club management committee or any individual shall have the right or power to contract out of any of the Laws of the Game as laid down by the International Bowling Board.

Regulating single-handed, pairs and triples games

70. The foregoing laws, where applicable, shall also apply to single-handed, pairs and triples games.

Spectators

71. Persons not engaged in the Game shall be situated clear of and beyond the limits of the rink of play, and clear of verges. They shall preserve an attitude of strict neutrality, and neither by word nor act disturb or advise the players.

Betting or gambling in connection with any game or games shall not be permitted or engaged in within the grounds of any constituent club.

Duties of Marker

72. (a) The Marker shall control the game in accordance with the IBB Basic Laws. He shall, before play commences, examine all bowls for the imprint of the IBB Stamp, or that of its National Association, such imprint to be clearly visible, and shall ascertain by measurement the width of the rink of play (see note after Law 73).

(b) He shall centre the jack, and

shall place a full-length jack 2 yards (1.84 metres) from the ditch.

(c) He shall ensure that the Jack is not less than 70 feet (21.35 metres) from the front edge of the mat, after it has been centred.

(d) He shall stand at one side of the rink, and to the rear of the jack.

(e) He shall answer affirmatively or negatively a player's inquiry as to whether a bowl is jack high. If requested, he shall indicate the distance of any bowl from the jack, or from any other bowl, and also, if requested, indicate which bowl he thinks is shot and/or the relative position of any other bowl.

(f) Subject to contrary directions from either opponent under Law 34, he shall mark all touchers immediately they come to rest, and remove chalk marks from non-touchers. With the agreement of both opponents he shall remove all dead bowls from the green and the ditch. He shall mark the positions of the jack and touchers which are in the ditch. (See Laws 33 and 40.)

(g) He shall not move, or cause to be moved, either jack or bowls until each player has agreed to the number of shots.

(h) He shall measure carefully all doubtful shots when requested by either player. If unable to come to a decision satisfactory to the players, he shall call in an Umpire. If an official Umpire has not been appointed, the marker shall select one. The decision of the Umpire shall be final.

(i) He shall enter the score at each end, and shall intimate to the players the state of the game. When the game is finished, he shall see that the score

Indicating the state of play to players and spectators is one of the marker's many duties. In the event of any dispute, the matter is referred to an umpire

card, containing the names of the players, is signed by the players, and disposed of in accordance with the rules of the competition.

Duties of Umpire

73. An Umpire shall be appointed by the Controlling Body of the Association, Club or Tournament Management Committee. His duties shall be as follows:

(a) He shall examine all bowls for the imprint of the IBB Stamp, or that of its National Association, and ascertain by measurement the width of the rinks of play.

(b) He shall measure any shot or shots in dispute, and for this purpose shall use a suitable measure. His decision shall be final.

(c) He shall decide all questions as to the distance of the mat from the ditch, and the jack from the mat.

(d) He shall decide as to whether or not jack and/or bowls are in play.

(e) He shall enforce the Laws of the Game.

(f) In World Bowls Championships and Commonwealth Games, the umpire's decision shall be final in respect of any breach of a Law, except that, upon questions relating to the meaning or interpretation of any Law, there shall be a right of appeal to the controlling body.

International Bowling Board By-Laws

Professional Bowler

All players are eligible for selection for Commonwealth Games except those whose principal source of Income is derived from playing the Game of Bowls.

Stamping of bowls

Manufacturers will be entitled to use an oval IBB stamp, to facilitate the imprint between the inner and outer rings of bowls. Imprints on running surfaces should be avoided wherever possible.

Glossary

Aiming point
The visual point towards which a bowler directs his bowl in order to achieve a desired result in the head. Some bowlers pick a spot on the bank behind the head, others try to imagine the shoulder of the arc and bowl to that point.

Athletic stance
A generally upright stance from which to make the delivery. The feet are in line with the shot, and it is simply a matter of bending the knees and stepping forward to ground the bowl. As modified to suit individual needs, this is by far the most common stance.

Bias
The running characteristics of a bowl. It can range from straightish (but not straighter than the Master Bowl) to 'bendy', with no limit to the 'bendiness'. The bowl's natural bias is predictably affected by playing conditions (state of the green, wind etc.).

Block shot
A short or shortish bowl whose purpose is to deprive the opponent of a clear route to the head.

Claw grip
Along with the cradle grip, one of the two conventional grips most generally employed in the British Isles. The thumb is positioned along or near the grip-line of the bowl (if it has one), and the bowl rests somewhat forward of the palm of the hand, on the fingers.

Cradle grip
As the name implies, a way of gripping the bowl so that it is cradled in the palm of the hand, with the thumb dropped. It is particularly suited to heavy conditions, because it allows maximum power with minimum effort.

Crouch stance
As immortalized by David Bryant, it is really a variation of the athletic stance – or, rather, a preamble to it. The depth of the crouch can vary, as feels comfortable, and its advocates claim that it improves the accuracy of line.

Ditching the jack
Driving the jack out of the head and into the ditch. If it comes to rest within the side boundaries of the rink it is a live jack and the end is therefore live. If it comes to rest outside the boundaries it is a dead jack and the end is declared dead and replayed.

Draw shot
The fundamental shot of bowls, where the object is to deliver the bowl to the jack. If the object is to draw to another position in the head, it is more properly described as a positional shot.

Drive shot
A power shot, the purpose of which is to disturb one or more bowls in the head so severely as to remove them from contention. It can be more or less full-blooded, depending upon requirements (and, to some extent, upon the temperament of the bowler).

Finger grip
An extreme version of the claw grip, where the bowl is held completely clear of the palm, with the thumb moving to the top of the bowl. It combines maximum sensitivity with minimum power, and is much favoured in the Southern Hemisphere, where the greens tend to run very fast.

Fixed stance
A method of delivery in which the front foot has completed its full step prior to delivery. The free hand steadies the body by gripping the knee or thigh of the leading leg. The price paid for this stability is a loss of power, and it is not generally favoured by able-bodied bowlers. For the disabled it may be the only choice, and it can be employed to remarkable effect.

Full-length jack
A jack delivered to within two yards of the front ditch. It is brought back to the two-yard mark and centred.

Green speed
The time, measured in seconds, that it takes a bowl to draw to a jack thirty yards from the front of the mat. The faster the green, the greater the time and therefore the higher the value accorded to the green speed. In the British Isles the average is ten to twelve seconds. In Australia and New Zealand it can approach and occasionally exceed twenty seconds.

Head
Theoretically, all the bowls that have been played to date and are resting within the confines of the rink. In

practice, the term is restricted to describe those bowls in the vicinity of the jack that appear likely to figure in the count when the end is completed.

IBB
The International Bowling Board, the governing body of the outdoor game. While the various national associations reserve the right to modify IBB regulations to suit local conditions, they all acknowledge its authority, and all international competitions take place under its auspices and in accordance with its Laws of the Game.

Jack high bowl
A bowl to one or other side of the jack, on a line horizontally with it.

Lignum vitae
The wood from which bowls used to be manufactured. Such bowls are generally regarded as obsolete, having been replaced by composition bowls.

Master Bowl
The international testing bowl which, under bench-test conditions, describes the minimum permitted arc. In order to qualify for any competition, all bowls must be similarly bench tested against that standard.

Positional shot
A bowl delivered to a predetermined spot in the head, other than to the jack or another bowl. It is a tactical shot, used to develop or strengthen the presence in the head so as to score in the end.

Rest shot
A shot that is drawn to a bowl in the head, the object being to rest against that bowl (generally the shot bowl) in such a way as to take the shot.

Running shots
All shots that are played with greater than draw weight, from a gentle tap and lie to a full-blooded drive.

Semi-fixed stance
A variation on the fixed stance, where the leading foot has only partially completed its step prior to delivery. The step is completed during the delivery. It is a more flexible style of delivery than the fixed, but less adaptable than the athletic.

Shot bowl
The bowl in the head lying nearest the jack.

Shoulder of the arc
The point at the extreme width of the curve described by a bowl in the course of its journey. From the shoulder of the arc the bowl curves inwards towards the head.

Tap and lie shot
A shot intended to replace an existing bowl (usually, but not always, an opponent's) by the bowl being delivered. It is played with slightly more than draw weight to the object bowl, so as to 'tap' it out of the way and 'lie' in its place.

Toucher
A bowl which, in its original course on the green, has made contact with the jack. Such a bowl is considered live even if it passes in to the ditch (within the boundaries of play), and it is marked with chalk to indicate its privileged status.

Tracking
A flattening of the grass along the principal lines of play within the rink. Tracking is to a greater or lesser extent inevitable during prolonged play, and the area affected runs quicker than its surroundings.

Trail shot
A necessarily difficult, but often telling shot which involves striking the jack and taking it through the head to a more favourable position.

Wick shot
A cannon shot, the object of which is to deflect the bowl from an existing bowl in a controlled direction (as a rule, towards the jack). Often regarded – and played – as a fluke, it can quite transform a seemingly hopeless position.

WIBC
The World Indoor Bowls Council, which is to the indoor game what the IBB is to the outdoor.

Yard on shot
A shot similar to the tap and lie, but played with more running (theoretically, a yard of running). The object is to shift another bowl (usually the shot bowl) well out of the way, without resorting to a drive shot.

Index

Acknowledgements

We would like to thank Eric Whitehead
for supplying the pictures on pages 106
and 123. The front cover photographs are
courtesy of Pascal Rondeau/Allsport. All
other photographs inside the book and on
the back cover are courtesy of *Bowls International* and their special photographer
Duncan Cubitt.

   We are also grateful to Bob Warters of
Bowls International for all his help and
co-operation.